AIKIDO'S HIDDEN
GROUND TECHNIQUES

BY

JOSE ANDRADE, M.D. AND DAVID NEMEROFF

Cover Story: Takemusu Aiki

The black and white photo on the cover was taken at the Noma Dojo in 1936 and shows Aikido Founder, Morihei Ueshiba, executing a ground defense technique (newaza) known as kata gatame, or shoulder lock. Most current aikidoka would be very surprised to see O'Sensei engaged in ground-fighting, but as discussed in this book, the founder of aikido viewed his art as transcending its traditional techniques. Aikido is more than a collection of moves, counters, and neutralization tactics. It is spontaneous martial action rooted in aiki principles, generated from total mental involvement in the current realistic situation.

On the cover the authors demonstrate ground techniques with a takemusu aiki flavor, which embodies Ueshiba's fundamental aikido principles. The techniques described within this text are simply an extension of Ueshiba's martial mastery, anchored and expressed through the Mukei No Ryu aikido paradigm.

Whether you are interested in aikido for its practical applications, personal transformation, as a form of meditation, or spiritual development, you must strive for a perpetual state of no-mind, undisturbed by thoughts, obstacles, or distractions. In this vein, keep in mind that to survive and thrive, it is invaluable to treat each encounter as a fresh situation, so that one can spontaneously adapt techniques to the specific scenario at hand. This will help facilitate the chances of survival in any confrontation and is what Morihei Ueshiba alludes to as the "Way of the Mountain Echo."

DEDICATION

We would like to dedicate this book to all of the judo, jujutsu, MMA, aikido and other ground grappling pioneers who cultivated this aspect of self-defense within the martial arts community.

Progress? When you have trained and when you have the unseen things look not for "Secret Teachings" For all is there, before your eyes.

Poetic Songs of the Way
Morihei Ueshiba (1883-1969)
Aiki News No. 46 March, 15, 1982

Acknowledgements

Grappling is a skill that has recently been a focus of martial arts practitioners and enthusiasts from around the world. We recognize all aikido instructors who have had the vision to include *newaza* (Ground Defense Techniques) in their training program.

We would like to acknowledge and thank all the people who had involvement with this book. We would like to thank Brian Crownover-Sensei for his guidance and professionalism as the editor of this book. He kept the project moving forward with a clear focus on the underlying vision of this endeavor. Brian brought his many years of experience in editorial work to bear on resolving creative differences between the authors and creating new literary vehicles for presenting newaza to the general public. Thank you for all your help and advice in seeing this work through from start to finish.

We also thank Oscar Sieres-Sensei and Yessica Andrade for their photographic and video recording skills and creativity in providing Andrade-Shihan's photographs. They are so essential to the instruction contained within this book. Their photographs clearly illustrate the intricacies of Aikido newaza as it is practiced in our Tenshinkai dojo and as it is employed in real-world scenarios. Thank you, Ramsey Veitch-Sensei, for your assistance with the video and photography for David Nemeroff-Shihan's part from Aikido Masters Self-Defense Academy.

We would like to give a very special thanks to Shizuya Sato (1929-2011), Hanshi tenth dan/founder of Nihon Jujutsu, nineth dan in judo, for his personal communication with Andrade-Shihan regarding historical Japanese information as well as his contributions to bringing budo to the limelight. He was also one of the founders of Kokusai Budoin, a prominent Japanese martial arts organization.

To the numerous uke who volunteered to participate in the photographic and video sessions, we say thank you for a job well-done. The following is a list of the uke who participated: Shane Baker, Wade Bailey, Ramsey Veitch, Grace Burns, Connor Fenstermaker, Javis Venini, Oscar Sieres-Sensei, David B. Parker-Sensei, Juan A. Armenteros, Frank Cruz-Sensei, Yessica Andrade, A.J. Gonzalez, Michael A. Blancero and Johnny Rivera.

Finally, we thank all of the instructors and students of aikido who share our desire to integrate advanced newaza techniques into their aikido curriculum. We believe that aikido has always been a superb vehicle for the transmission of newaza. We welcome receiving your communications, including questions, concerning your experiences in promoting aikido newaza.

Table of Contents

Dedication iii
Acknowledgements v
Preface 1
Introduction 5
Samurai, Bushido and MMA: How We Got Here 9
A Tale of Two Masters: Jigoro Kano and Morihei Ueshiba 15
The Great Controversy: Tradition vs. Adapting to Modern Times 19
Is It Jujutsu or Aikido? 25
Calling All Grapplers! 29
Getting the Most from Newaza Training 31
Mukei No Ryu Aikido: An Overview 33
Fundamental Aikido Techniques 39
Strategic Insights of Mukei No Ryu Aikido 43
The Clinch: A Likely Transition From Tachiwaza to Newaza 47
Mastering Kuzushi: The Art of Breaking Balance 53
Exploring Aikido Principles with The Sangen 59
Newaza—Not! 65
Newaza for Children 67
The Importance of Posture and Stances 73
Mukei No Ryu's Categorization of Newaza 77
Ground Defense Positions 79
Newaza Mechanics and the Combination Lock 85
Suwariwaza and Hanmi Handachiwaza 92
Takin' It to the Street 118
Concluding Thoughts: 175
Glossary 177
About The Dvd: 185
About The Authors 189
Martial Arts Works by the Authors 195

Without the Slightest opening nor the least thought of the enemy and his encircling swords. Step in and cut!

> Poetic Songs of the Way
> Morihei Ueshiba (1883-1969)
> Aiki News No. 46 March, 15, 1982

Preface

Ah, the big city! A claustrophobic throng of the masses are out and going about their business and pleasure. Buses stop at intersections, hiss and disgorge passengers onto the sidewalk. Bright neon lights advertising fine dining, bars, stores and adult entertainment flash and shine demanding your attention. Smells of car exhaust, ethnic foods, people and who knows what else assault your nose. The big city is a cacophony of sensory stimulation and has a fast-paced rhythm of life all its own. Opportunity beckons and danger lurks nearby.

Cities often contain a narrow strip of wealth and commerce constituting a veneer of high civilization. Step to either side of the city's spine, however, and you can find yourself in a dark world, a world in which desperate people do what they must to survive. Living in old, dilapidated brick tenements with metal fire escapes, theirs is a land of economic blight and gang violence.

Suppose that you are out for a walk on the city's main street and being unfamiliar with the surroundings, you make a fateful wrong turn and wind up in the world one block over. The sights and sounds in which you were immersed have vanished. You stand on a poorly lit sidewalk. To either side of the street stand the old brick tenements and abandoned brick warehouses.

Your internal alarms are ringing. You should not be here! Turning around, you see a shadowy human shape appear merely feet away. You instinctively move to the right to give the person a wide berth. He anticipates your move and lunges toward you and throws you down. One moment you are soaring in the air; a second later your back slams onto the sidewalk. Your breath is taken away, and your back feels the blunt force-trauma from the concrete. The attacker has mounted you and is ready to begin a "ground and pound" on your head. What do you do? How do you defend yourself? To what extremes will you go to survive?

To answer the last question, you can and should go to any extreme necessary to survive and thrive. Assuming you are not the aggressor, you are under no obligation to forswear a violent response to an attack that will, in all likelihood, lead to great bodily harm or even to death. You are not obligated to adopt a pacifist philosophy in which you allow the violence against you because of being told that you cannot solve the problem of violence with more violence. You are not obligated to "turn the other cheek." That will only bring harm to both of your cheeks. Like any life form on this planet, you have the right to self-defense. Evolution has endowed each animal with its own, often times amazing techniques of defense against predators. Humans are no different except that we have more flexibility in creating and utilizing various means of defense.

Nowadays, martial arts schools do not usually train students to deal with the brutality and the unpredictability of a street fight. In a street fight, there are no rules. Anything goes and usually does. In the world of sport fighting such as mixed martial arts (MMA), the contestants must obey rules preventing joint breaking, eye gouging, elbow strikes, groin strikes and other harmful and/or deadly techniques of hand-to-hand combat. In a martial art school, one will punch and kick air, spar with an opponent wearing protective gear and learn submission techniques that force the opponent to tap out, all in order to avoid injury to the students. This is as it should be. The point is that during a street fight the attacker must be neutralized and incapacitated to the extent that he or she is no longer a threat to your survival. However, to defend yourself, any techniques you learned through martial training will have to be extended or instantly modified on the spot to ensure a positive outcome.

So, to answer the question, "What do you do?" in response to the scenario presented above, reexamine the situation. You were taken from a standing position and forcefully placed in a supine position. Your head, chest and arms are exposed to probable harm. The attacker's position on top of your chest and abdomen has you immobilized. The attacker is in a position to strike you continuously. Escape seems difficult, if not impossible.

We propose that practical combative newaza (ground techniques) is the most effective means of defending yourself and prevailing in this type of situation. Newaza can be executed when a tactical conflict results with both attacker and defender on the ground. The repertoire of aikido newaza covers all situations regardless of whether the attacker or the defender is on top. The ground techniques conclude with either a choke, a hyperextension (bar) to an arm or leg, a pin, some other submission or an incapacitating strike.

This book presents aikido, the Japanese martial art created by Morihei Ueshiba, as an ideal context in which to study and practice newaza. Aikido is a defensive, noncompetitive martial art known for its empty-hand techniques (taijutsu) that bear a close relationship to sword movements. These immobilizations, take downs, pins and submissions are practiced by pairs of students commonly in standing positions (tachiwaza), in seated positions (suwariwaza) and in a one standing, one seated position (hanmi handachiwaza).

Aikido is characterized by using the flowing movement directed from one's anatomical and energetic center point (hara), harmonizing with the energy of the attacker and redirecting it. Then, the aikidoka neutralizes the attack by creating off balance and controlling the attacker through pain compliance. The highest form of aikido (takemusu aiki) occurs when one can respond to an attack adeptly with an agile mind free from the requirements imposed by specific predetermined techniques. It is really a state of mind in which one is perfectly present in the moment and able to respond immediately and creatively to a rapidly changing dynamic event. Adaptability and fluidity of movement in the spirit of takemusu aiki (spontaneous movements drawing from the natural flow of energy in the universe) should be the hallmark of any aikido style and/or newaza practice. The ability to perform newaza freely in accordance with takemusu aiki, when necessary, is the answer to the questions posed by the preceding tactical scenario.

Many schools of aikido do not consider newaza to be "traditional" and therefore do not instruct their students in the practice. On the other hand, Andrade-Shihan, founder of Mukei No Ryu aikido, freely expresses the importance of using any and all types of self-defense practice, including newaza, to give students of this art the greatest possible repertoire of techniques and applications for their total defense of self.

A few appropriate considerations are offered here. The reader will not become proficient in newaza or any other martial techniques from this book, any similar books or videos. Only through steady, committed training at an authentic martial arts school under a qualified instructor can you learn and master the art of newaza, or any other martial art or skill for that matter.

However, this book can serve as an important starting point for anyone contemplating the study of aikido. Seek out a qualified instructor who teaches aikido newaza with kindness, an open mind and enthusiasm. Keep in mind that your education is most important. Formulate goals and take the destiny of your aikido development into your own hands.

Pour your spirit and heart into daily technical training

To approach the many through a single principle

This is "The Way of the Fighting Man."

> Poetic Songs of the Way
> Morihei Ueshiba (1883-1969)
> Aiki News No. 46 March, 15, 1982

Introduction

The popularity of the Ultimate Fighting Championship (UFC) and Mixed Martial Arts (MMA) has propelled newaza (ground techniques) to the forefront of the martial arts world and into the media's limelight. More than ever before, people are seeing the necessity of this important skill. However, many people do not realize that another popular traditional martial art, aikido, can have a distinct method of newaza as part of its style. This book presents an aspect of the martial arts that has often been neglected, even intentionally excluded, by much of the aikido community.

Students of aikido must have a sense of self-preservation, awareness and knowledge of the dynamics of physical violence. Those whose naïve image of an attacker elicits images of beautiful, graceful movement and harmonious blending of energy in compassion and non-resistance will experience shock and disillusionment when the outcome of the assault is bloody, ugly and brutal. Aikido's non-fighting conflict resolution philosophy will probably not sway a predator toward peace and reconciliation.

To survive and thrive in a street fight, the aikidoka must be free from orthodox views of approved stances and techniques. Forget about peaceful resolution, spiritual growth and enlightenment because such interests do not limit the person attacking. If you choose to study newaza, keep in mind that ground fighting is a serious combative skill set for self-defense that is useful in certain, but not all, situations. Nonetheless, any serious martial artist has a need and personal obligation to adapt and expand their training methods to encompass the rewarding art of aikido newaza.

We teach these and other techniques, but it is up to students how hard they want to train. Training must be done with intensity, but safety is also a consideration. There must be a balance. By training too softly, there is a lack of realism that will leave you ill prepared for the dangers of the street. However, by training too intensely, a student is at high risk of injury. Plenty of fighters who train for the ring end up with concussions, broken bones, brain damage, and even death. Remember, the martial arts are meant to build you up, not break you down, so consideration must be given to how much trauma one's body should endure. Don't get us wrong, the body must be physically challenged and some pain should be experienced to understand what is the right amount of pressure to apply on a technique as well as how hard to strike.

We just want those who train to realize that longevity for practitioners should last beyond one or two fights.

One might say that if it is not taken to extremes then you are never truly prepared. We would argue that if you injure yourself so you cannot practice any more then what is the point? People go to the gun range to practice, but does that mean that if they have a gun they should kill people? That would be an extreme situation, correct? The same goes for the martial arts.

The purpose of this book is to emphasize the practical self-defense aspect of aikido through the practice of newaza. As the scenario outlined in the **Preface** shows, sometimes there is no choice but for an altercation to "go to the ground." Not studying newaza could have dire consequences. A study of the art of aikido should not leave its devotees unprotected and unable to respond effectively to any street situation. To be a complete martial artist, one must be versed in all areas of self-defense, including defenses while on the ground. Being proficient in newaza can alter the course of such a tactical situation. Those with knowledge of ground fighting are more likely to emerge victorious, or at least alive.

The newaza demonstrated in this text is a natural extension of aikido's core set of techniques. So, some of these techniques are presented first in order to afford you with the ability to identify them and give you a better idea of how standing techniques are a reflection of ones on the ground. Keep in mind however, that within the context of Mukei No Ryu aikido, newaza is more than simply learning a collection of locks, takedowns or throws. Effectiveness comes from the understanding and internalization of aikido principles and fundamental body movements. In this light, aikido strategies can be applied to any situation, whether a person is standing or on the ground. Therefore, in order to grasp aikido newaza it is important for the reader to be exposed to the philosophy as well as the techniques. These principles will be explicated in more depth throughout this book.

This book presents Mukei No Ryu aikido newaza in three progressive phases. Firstly, it recognizes that aikido has always offered a basic level of newaza through the practices of suwariwaza (attacker and defender are seated) and hanmi handachiwaza (attacker standing, defender seated). The attacker delivers standardized, stylized strikes and the defender utilizes classic aikido immobilizations and takedowns followed by pins and submissions. Movements from a position of sitting on one's heels (seiza) are made by knee-walking (shikko). While some aikido schools have viewed suwariwaza as simply a traditional exercise, it provides a grounded platform from which to practice Basic Newaza. Later in this text, several newaza applications from suwariwaza and hanmi handachiwaza will be presented.

Secondly, Mukei No Ryu aikido newaza contains another phase, traditional newaza, in which attacker and defender begin from standing positions. Traditional immobilizations and takedowns are employed to set the stage leading into effective pins and submissions while on the ground. Like all traditional aikido styles, the defender blends with the attack to attain and then maintain control throughout the technique. A series of traditional newaza will be taught following a presentation of the basic elements of successful newaza.

Thirdly, Mukei No Ryu aikido newaza takes ground fighting to a new and combative level that transcends the standard aikido curriculum. Advanced aiki-newaza is designed for that street encounter gone wrong. When control of a chaotic situation is difficult and an attack puts your life in jeopardy there are ground techniques available that will give you a fighting chance to survive and prevail. While advanced aiki-newaza may, in some instances, resemble jujutsu, each aikido ground technique applies the principles unique to aikido.

The companion DVD demonstrates and explains each technique of basic newaza, traditional newaza and advanced aiki-newaza. During the instruction of suwariwaza and traditional newaza, the instructors wear the traditional hakama (skirt-like pant). Due to the need for complete visibility of the sometimes complex and close-in techniques of advanced aiki-newaza, the instructor does not wear the hakama. No disrespect of aikido etiquette is implied or intended. In any dojo, the use or nonuse of the hakama is at the discretion of the instructor.

From a Mukei No Ryu perspective, the study of newaza complements what aikido already has to offer. Training in newaza strengthens the body, opens the mind to new martial possibilities, improves flexibility and increases both endurance and overall cardiovascular function. Ground training develops and requires great physical stamina while challenging the mind to adapt to constantly changing circumstances. Like any vigorous physical activity, participants should make sure that they are healthy enough to handle the extra activity. If you are unsure about whether your body can deal with the physical demands of newaza, consult a qualified physician. Also, no training should be attempted without the supervision of a qualified instructor.

We hope you find the Mukei No Ryu aikido approach to newaza helpful in presenting a new phase of your martial arts training. There is always more to learn and apply as you develop into a true aikidoka. As always, be heart-smart and control your own destiny.

Even when a single enemy has called you out

Be on your best guard

An entire host of the foe

Is on your left, your right, in front and behind.

Poetic Songs of the Way
Morihei Ueshiba (1883-1969)
Aiki News No. 46 March, 15, 1982

Samurai, Bushido and MMA: How We Got Here

In recent decades, martial arts awareness and practice has boomed worldwide. More than anywhere else in the world, the United States of America has become the melting pot of martial arts. All styles of grappling have experienced resurgence due to the results of a certain modern form of martial entertainment. It began on November 12, 1993 with the first pay-per-view live broadcast event of mixed martial arts (MMA) by the Ultimate Fighting Championship (UFC). Royce Gracie won the tournament via submission using a rear neck choke. This victory opened the eyes of many in the martial arts world to the effectiveness of a grappling style. The name of the art, "Gracie Jiujitsu," founded by Helio Gracie, gained international recognition. The popularity of MMA has flourished, in part, by televised events such as Strike Force, King of the Ring, Affliction and others. The dominance of grappling styles in the ring has caused promoters to organize events such as K-1 for strikers only.

Many of the styles and techniques used by MMA fighters can be traced back to the time of the samurai in Japan. The samurai were the warrior class of feudal and imperial Japan. Today, martial arts schools dedicated to spreading Japanese arts may teach versions of traditional Japanese grappling and striking arts. MMA schools teach truncated, eclectic variations of these same Japanese martial arts. So inquiring minds might wonder how an MMA fighter would fare against a samurai in combat. In other words, can a student learn effective self-defense in schools teaching traditional martial arts? The ramifications of this question impact newaza training for modern aikido, jujutsu, aikijujutsu and judo schools. To answer these questions requires a more complete understanding of the samurai and their training.

Between the eleventh and fifteenth centuries CE in Japan, methodical training in preparation for war, including weapons manufacturing, flourished in martial styles known as Ryu-ha. Ryu-ha were the creations of samurai, ronin or even common people. These ryu-ha specialized in different survival arts extracted and refined from battlefield experience. Specific examples of these ryu-ha include Tenshin Shōden Katori Shintō-ryū, Kashima Shinryu, and Maniwa Nen-ryu. Other general catagories of ryu-ha are the warrior art of the sword (kenjutsu), the art of archery (kyujutsu), horsemanship (bajutsu), javelin (sojutsu), throwing bladed objects (shurikenjutsu), staff (bojutsu), swimming (suijutsu) and grappling methods, with or without weapons (kumi-uchi) evolved into formal fighting methods by warriors mastering the essentials drawn from every aspect of combat.

As ancient Japanese martial arts developed into modern traditional Japanese martial ways, there arose a delineation between martial arts whose names had the suffix jutsu (art of war) and arts' names having the suffix do (arts of enlightenment). Such jutsu arts include jujutsu (gentle art of war), kenjutsu (sword art of war), aikijujutsu (internal energy gentle art of war), karatejutsu (empty hand art of war), and so on. These arts of war were, without exception, predecessors to their respective *do* arts of judo (gentle way), kendo (way of the sword), aikido (way of harmonious energy) and karate-do (way of the empty hand). In general, jutsu arts were concerned almost exclusively with victory in battle, practical applications for warfare and the function and coordination of group combat. Do arts were designed to fulfill spiritual needs and to provide persons with personal self defense training.

The samurai had a substantial influence on the emergence of the Japanese martial way. These samurai were regarded as the dominant social class from Japan's Edo period until early in the Meiji era. Whether as frontiersmen, border guards or protectors of the emperor, these elite warriors rose in power to dominate the emperors they were supposed to serve. Although ultimate authority rested with the emperors, there were times when they were puppets obliged to delegate their authority to the shogunate, or military rule of Japan. The warlord family (daimyo) provided the country with fifteen shoguns comprising the Edo shogunate. The shogun ruled Japan in an authoritarian fashion in the name of the emperor. From the Western Middle Ages until the nineteenth century, they remained the dominant force by seizing control of Japan in the emperor's name. The Tokugawa dynasty was the last line of shoguns. They endured as victors over an expansive period of more than two centuries.

The samurai were the embodiment of Japanese martial traditions. At the center of these traditions was Zen spirituality and the worldview of the samurai. A samurai's physical and mental training required rigid adherence and obedience to their instructors' commands leaving little or no explication of the rationale behind any given technique. The result of this non-reflective training was each samurai's unification of mind, body and spirit with the universe, or at least with the will of his leader.

The samurai were unconcerned with compassion as we define it. For thousand years war was their profession. They trained rigorously throughout their lives, preparing themselves in every manner of combat without feeling a need for glamour or glory. They adhered to the unwritten code of Bushido (way of the warrior), the stringent ethical and spiritual code that took shape in seventeenth century Japan. The samurai's bravery, serenity and way of life, especially toward matters of life and death, were the product of their strict devotion and full commitment to the teachings and practices of Zen Buddhism and their absolute loyalty to their warlords.

Many samurai practiced Zen Buddhism. One might wonder why warriors would practice a philosophy of peace when their entire life's training prepared them for war. Actually, Zen training provided the samurai with some social refinement (tea ceremony, calligraphy, meditation) and, at the same time, removed the mental distance between an event and the samurai's response. For the samurai, "peace" was not the cessation of violence; rather, it was committing an act of violence in a non-critical, unified state of mind, body and will.

According to Zen master Taisen Deshimaru in "The Zen Way To Martial Arts" he states, Bushido, the way of the samurai, grew out of the fusion of Buddhism and Shintoism. This way can be summarized in seven essential principles:

1. Gi: the right decision, taken with equanimity, the right attitude, the truth; 'When we must die, we must die.' Rectitude.

2. Yu: bravery tinged with heroism.

3. Jin: universal love, benevolence toward mankind; compassion.

4. Rei: right action—a most essential quality, courtesy.

5. Makoto: utter sincerity; truthfulness.

6. Melyo: honor and glory.

7. Chugo: devotion, loyalty.

The way of the warrior and the goal of a Zen monk coincided in mastery of self.

The samurai were not just the epitome of a spiritual warrior; they were renowned as fierce, merciless killing machines. They were respected icons in Japanese culture because they embodied the Japanese spirit. Through repetitive, face-to-face, hostile opposition encountered amidst the conflict of war, the samurai were able to perfect their martial techniques. Their survival was possible only by eliminating any and all flawed techniques. Any style of practice that did not produce a purposeful, vital function suffered the same fate. Survival of the fittest was the order of the day. Later, those techniques that worked were enshrined in kata (choreographed martial movements). That way, future warriors could be trained in the most effective combat techniques. For the samurai, he was the product of his training and his fearless spirit was as hard as the steel of his sword. His sword was his soul.

As Japan entered the modern world, the samurai were prohibited by national decree from wearing swords. This struck a blow more powerful than any martial art technique at the very essence of what it meant to be a warrior. Without his sword, the samurai could not pursue a life dedicated to advancement in the study of do. As a result of the decree, all Japanese martial arts suffered a decline even while some martial training continued.

As Japan entered the twentieth century, the samurai's social and military status changed. Their military function was no longer considered to be of much value against modern arms. Technological developments left the samurai behind and they never recovered. Many samurai who were unprepared for peace and disenchanted with the oppressiveness of the political order, rebelled and fought against their emperor. Others simply adapted to the times and opportunities or faded into the general population, unemployed and impoverished. Some, in order to save their honor, committed a form of ritual suicide by disembowelment (seppuku). Nevertheless, the values and ideals of Bushido were preserved and integrated throughout Japanese culture during the transition into modernity and western influence.

After examining the past, it is obvious that MMA practitioners are not the pioneers of grappling that many view them to be. Professional wrestling as a sport/entertainment has been around decades longer. Popular grappling arts such as Brazilian jiu jitsu, judo and so on evolved from traditional Japanese jujutsu, which in turn, derived from centuries-old methods of Asian wrestling. Newaza was relevant in the past during times of war. It remains relevant in military hand-to-hand combat, civilian personal self-defense, and sport/entertainment.

So how would a samurai fare against a modern MMA fighter? The samurai held a totally different and more complete concept of MMA. Their training incorporated whole systems of techniques representing different aspects of combat. In contrast, today's MMA fighters frequently learn small parts of various styles of punching, kicking, grappling, and submissions. For example, a samurai family-style was composed of complete systems of separate arts such as throwing, grappling, striking, skills with weapons, and so on while teaching the same fundamental principles of combat and spirituality throughout them all. Different techniques were unified into a coherent ryu-ha. The samurai family's system incorporated the same underlying philosophy and methodology of combat that included footwork, blocking methods, evasive concepts and proper mental preparation such as Zen meditation practices. Such a martial philosophy took the trainee longer to master, but he knew that what was taught worked on the battlefield.

The spirituality of war demanded that the samurai be free from distracting passions. He was not concerned with following fight rules, obeying a referee, winning trophies, or gaining a fan club. The samurai was conditioned to be unconcerned with his death as he engaged in mortal combat against single or multiple attackers, with or without weapons. The samurai strived for sincerity of heart, self-control and self-perfection, not self-protection.

The life-or-death stakes of actual combat, the mental discipline, and the comprehensive martial training made the samurai a more formidable warrior than the modern MMA fighter. These parameters made the samurai more capable of defending himself if challenged to a fight or attacked without warning. In comparison, this does not necessarily make the mma fighter incompetent or free from the risk of injuries during a competitive bout. For us, it is difficult, if not impossible, to duplicate all of the samurai's physical and mental training. We can only hope that if attacked, something deep inside our person will respond appropriately and effectively to enable our survival. That something deep inside is the body-mind.

The body-mind is not constrained by critical awareness, doubts, or thoughts of any kind. It is that within us that acts! Long-term training in aikido, including newaza, can teach the body-mind to react in selfless defense against an attacker and prevail.

Mobilize all your powers through Aiki

Build a beautiful world

And a secure peace.

Poetic Songs of the Way
Morihei Ueshiba (1883-1969)
Aiki News No. 46 March, 15, 1982

A Tale of Two Masters:
Jigoro Kano and Morihei Ueshiba

When discussing the historical development of newaza, the contributions of one man loom large. Dr. Jigoro Kano (1860-1938) created judo, the way of gentleness, during the Meiji era, a time of revolutionary changes in Japanese society. Judo is mainly based on unarmed combat techniques used in feudal warfare by Japanese warriors. Jigoro Kano combined elements of old styles of jujutsu ryu-ha such as Teinosuke yagi jujutsu, Tenjin shinyo ryu (striking and grappling techniques), Kito-ryu (throwing techniques) and others. As a professor of education, he added his own principles and philosophy into a coherent and effective standing and ground fighting martial art.

Judo Founder Jigoro Kano

In 1882, at twenty-two years of age, Jigoro Kano founded the Kodokan Judo Institute in Tokyo, Japan. (Ko-do-kan translates as practice-way-hall.) The institute became the world center for judo instruction and certification. As part of Dr. Kano's life-long pursuit of learning, he visited dojo throughout Japan, even studying secret techniques from various ryu-ha, in order to enhance his judo.

One reason he created judo was to improve the negative views harbored by the public about martial arts being a violent and out-dated practice. Dr. Kano also developed his art as a less aggressive means of training in the efficient use of energy and in the importance of proper timing in the execution of techniques. As part of his vision, he modified and/or excluded combat techniques that were dangerous and focused on those techniques that could be performed safely on a person who was allowed to resist.

From the hub that was the Kodokan, judo was disseminated throughout Japan and the world. The founder promoted his creation as a complete physical and mental self-defense system and as a philosophy of the art of daily living. While Dr. Kano envisioned his art as a spiritual endeavor, after World War II, judo was more often promoted as an international sport. Dr. Kano's judo eventually became a mandatory sport of study in all Japanese schools, and judo was included as an official Olympic sport in 1964 and remains a highly popular martial art.

Some judo students try to practice the art as Dr. Kano originally conceived it. Most others practice it as a westernized sport. Judo was a major influence on martial arts luminaries such as Kenji Tomiki, Minoru Mochizuki and Sato Shizuya.

Aikido Founder, O'Sensei, Morihei Ueshiba

During October, 1930, Dr. Kano, and some of his students, including Kyuzo Mifune[1], one of Dr. Kano's top disciples, visited Morihei Ueshiba (1883-1969). After watching Ueshiba perform his Aikido, Dr. Kano called the exhibition "my ideal Budo." He decided to send some of his top students including Tomiki[2] and Mochizuki-Sensei[3] to train under Ueshiba. Kenji Tomiki-Sensei, founder of Tomiki-ryu aikido, incorporated the competitive aspects of judo into his aikido, which is referred to as aikido kyogi, or competitive aikido. Tomiki-Sensei also founded the Japan Aikido Association. Mochizuki-Sensei founded Yoseikan Budo circa 1931, after approximately one year as a live-in student of Morihei Ueshiba. His style includes elements of judo, aikido, karate and kobudo. Both Tomiki-Sensei and Mochizuki-Sensei remained loyal to Dr. Jigoro Kano.

---

1. A YouTube video shows Kyuzo Mifune performing magnificent judo that appears similar to O'Sensei's aikido. He was granted Judo Meijin, tenth dan by Kokusai Budoin.
2. Kenji Tomiki earned the rank of eighth dan in both Judo and Aikido by the founders of each art.
3. Minoru Mochizuki earned the rank of seventh dan in Judo under Dr, Kano and the rank of tenth dan in Aikido by Kokusai Budoin. His budo did not involve competition.

What spawned Dr. Kano's interest in Ueshiba's aikido? Was it Ueshiba's technical expertise and/or the lack of competition? Was it the ethical implications of aikido that seemed similar to his original intentions? Did Dr. Kano have regrets about how his own art developed as a sport? These valid questions continue to intrigue many martial artists today.

The answers to the above questions depend on one's point of view. Certain traditionalist aikido circles that remain non-proponents of judo and other martial arts believe that Dr. Kano regretted the creation of judo because his art was inferior to Ueshiba's aikido. More likely, the so-called ideal budo referred to the ethical, moral and spiritual implications that both arts shared—avoidance of injury and creation of a more peaceful society. Whichever your point of view on this matter, it is certainly true that it takes a humble master to know another. Dr. Jigoro Kano and Morihei Ueshiba greatly admired each other and possessed many positive attributes in common.

While living in Tanabe, young Ueshiba studied Dr. Kano's kodokan judo for a short time under Kiyoichi Takagi. Morihei Ueshiba also studied Kito-ryu jujutsu and Tenjin shinyo-ryu jujutsu as did Dr. Kano. Ueshiba and Dr. Kano encouraged their students to study other martial arts with a variety of teachers. After World War II, Morihei Ueshiba implemented judo's belt system and its issuing of instructor ranks (dan). Both Ueshiba and Dr. Kano followed the Omoto-kyo religion of Onisaburo Deguchi, a similar spiritual vision guiding their paths. Dr. Kano and Morihei Ueshiba modernized elements of old styles of jujutsu and aikijujutsu to create judo and aikido, respectively. Neither martial artist ever stopped their relentless cultivation of martial excellence, perfection of character and spiritual development. One can see how, with the similar roots of these masters, newaza could have been included in both aikido and judo systems.

The connection between judoka and aikidoka continues to this day. Since becoming the United State Judo Association (USJA) Aikido Chairman in March 2010, Andrade-Shihan has actively promoted aikido through clinics and demonstrations in Florida, California and Indiana. According to USJA Growing Judo Online Magazine, October 2011, during the September 2011 America's Cup Judo Championship in Pendleton, Indiana, many participants expressed interest in learning and incorporating aikido principles into their judo and jujitsu. During the aikido seminar, wrist locks, strikes at vital points (atemi) and proper body movements (irimi, or entering, tenkan, or turning, and so on) were demonstrated. In addition, the training covered defense techniques against kicks (keriwaza), jabs, unarmed technique (taijutsu), variation techniques (henkawaza), countering techniques (kaeshiwaza) and armed techniques (bukiwaza). In response, many senior students and instructors expressed a strong desire to study traditional Japanese budo through aikido and to revive original practical elements of judo, which have disappeared during the natural evolution of the art.

Concerning Morihei Ueshiba and his art, it was during 1942 when aikido was recognized officially as the name of Ueshiba's art. Prior to that time, the martial art was called Kobukan aikibudo, Ueshiba-ryu jujutsu and Tenshi aikibudo. Ueshiba was always searching for a name that expressed the essence of his art. For a time, he considered replacing the name aikido with Takemusu Aiki, the spontaneous emergence of technique from the wisdom of the body-mind.

Obviously, aikido, judo and aiki-jujutsu share a history of martial development with the later martial arts drawing upon and transforming the earlier arts. As practitioners of these arts continue to borrow techniques from each other to fill a perceived need, the ideal of what constitutes traditional aikido will necessarily change. In fact, aikido has already spawned numerous schools of aikido that teach different techniques and different ways of performing such techniques. Yet there are those who would deny newaza status in aikido. This topic is addressed next.

The Great Controversy:
Tradition vs. Adapting to Modern Times

Traditionally, many ryu-ha, including aikido, originated as comprehensive martial arts in their own right as a result of a lifetime of study and evaluation of various martial techniques. Many different elements essential to relatively modern arts were borrowed from other older koryu disciplines, integrated into a new system and presented as valid Do arts. At this point, the new arts became the foundation of new traditions. For example, the founders of karate-do, judo, aikido, and other arts created their own martial arts after having studied several older systems under the tutelage of some great teachers. Following a separation from their teachers and their earlier traditions, the innovators established their own new traditions. This process, known as shuhari, has repeated many times over. Morihei Ueshiba studied Daito-ryu aikijujutsu under Sokaku Takeda, taught the art and gave rank in the art. As we know, he went on to found aikido, a martial art derived from Takeda's Daito-ryu and other arts.

Along with shuhari comes a kind of convenient forgetfulness. Those who stress following tradition by not permitting any "unapproved" techniques do not acknowledge the facts that their traditions are not as ancient as they believe them to be while formerly innovative arts have become ossified. With regard to teaching newaza, some aikido traditionalists insist that ground techniques have no place in the art. They can cite a lack of a comprehensive newaza curriculum in the founder's and his immediate disciples' instruction. Others see a need to keep aikido relevant to the times and societies in which it is taught and to evolve the art technically. These aikidoka are likely to reinterpret the art in such a way that newaza can be seen as an extension of what already exists in aikido. Still others grab any technique that may seem useful and form an art that has no internal coherence, but is effective for self-defense. So, can and should newaza be a part of aikido curricula? And if so, how?

The question concerning the inclusion of newaza begins with the founder of aikido, Morihei Ueshiba (O'Sensei) and his early students. No martial artists' reputations in Japan or elsewhere rivaled that of O'Sensei for his martial expertise, his spiritual journey, pursuit of peace, and his creation of an ethical version of self-defense. After a devastating war with the United States of America, his intention was to heal humankind. These goals became ever clearer as he matured and further developed his art. Watch and compare his initial aikido techniques in his older films and photographs to what he demonstrated in the more recent ones. He pushed the boundaries of what was considered traditional martial arts by taking what he learned from various technical styles and infusing them with a profoundly moral and compassionate ethic.

Some aikidoka think they have been practicing the same aikido as Morihei Ueshiba. However, since no person has ever followed with exact precision and total devotion the complete path of O'Sensei's aikido journey, no one can claim to be his equal. As much as we may try to emulate Morihei Ueshiba and our personal teachers, the aikido we practice and the way we live is our own. This is not a bad thing. Each person has their own set of values and embodies unique characteristics, experiences, opinions and ideologies. In as much as Morihei Ueshiba was deeply involved with ancient Japanese religion and other spiritual matters, it is not possible for us to fully experience his odyssey and see all aspects of the universe through his eyes. Our blindness prevents us from realizing this truth. As long as we maintain the technical principles and concepts inherent to Ueshiba's art, we are staying on the path.

Most of O'Sensei's disciples did not spend as many years studying directly under his tutelage as one might think. Those who were with him longest were not present for his entire lifetime. O'Sensei did not spend much time at his school (dojo) demonstrating aikido techniques to his students. He was often away, spreading his spiritual message on his travels across Japan. As time went by, his trips increased in frequency. Even when home, he partook in other activities such as farming. At the dojo, his disciples endured long hours of what they considered tedious, incomprehensible lectures on spiritual, theological and metaphysical matters that no one seemed to understand. O'Sensei was increasingly often preoccupied by his religious beliefs and often concentrated on his own spiritual endeavors. It is unlikely that O'Sensei was able to pass on his abilities with ki (internal energy) since none of his students were able to duplicate some of the extraordinary martial actions that required a highly refined and powerful use of ki.

Highly regarded and technically skilled Japanese aikido luminaries such as Koichi Tohei, Gozo Shioda, Shoji Nishio, Morihiro Saito, Seigo Yamaguchi and others considered practical masters in their own right, interpreted their experiences and advanced technical aikido skills their own way. Although they were all instrumental in fostering the development of aikido, none can claim to be the sole authority of traditional aikido. They created unique styles very different from Morihei Ueshiba's traditional aikido. Their ability to forge new ideas, practices, patterns and relationships and to expound upon what they learned made them true visionaries. They were certainly influenced by O'Sensei's evolving style, and their styles of aikido differed, depending on where and when they were taught. For example, pre-World War II films showed O'Sensei's aikido to be more rigid, harder, and "militant." Long after this war, his style became softer and even more flowing. So, from its inception, aikido styles transformed as times, instructors and students all changed.

With this historical commentary in mind, we return to the practice of newaza. There is an ongoing controversy among aikidoka as to whether newaza should be a part of an aikido curriculum. Some approve of newaza's inclusion in the context of suwariwaza and hanmi handachiwaza. Others claim that ground techniques are unorthodox and should not be included in aikido instruction. Consider that once Ueshiba had developed his reputation as a skilled fighter, martial artists and common street thugs traveled from far and near to challenge him. He fought masters in many arts, including grapplers. So doesn't it make sense that he had some understanding of newaza technique if he defeated others skilled at ground fighting?

Tradition has been defined as the handing down of statements, beliefs, legends, customs, and so on from generation to generation by word of mouth and/or through various practices. For those who claim that newaza is not a part of aikido, there exists an old black-and-white video of O'Sensei performing newaza. He starts on his knees and is attacked from behind by a standing opponent (hanmi handachi). He finishes with newaza. During the technique, he proceeds to roll onto his back while grabbing the attacker's head by wrapping his feet around the attacker's neck, and throwing him forward. That is newaza. One can argue that if what O'Sensei does is traditional by definition, then newaza must be traditional aikido. This same technique is also found in the book *Budo: Teachings of the Founder of Aikido,* by Morihei Ueshiba, page 128.

In 1936, more than 1,200 technical photos of Aikido Founder Morihei Ueshiba and his student Shigemi Yonekawa were taken at the Noma Dojo. Part of the photo collection of Ueshiba's prewar art represented a transition phase between Daito-ryu Aikijujutsu and modern aikido. This photo collection contains many newaza images, performed by Morihei Ueshiba at around age fifty-three in a youtube video tittled Prewar And Postwar Aikido published by Marius Vladicka (You Tube link **https://www.youtube.com/watch?v=NOd4WmdjbAI**).

Just for good measure, another newaza photo from the Noma Dojo was posted on the AikiWeb on July 26, 2008 by Dangayan Singkaw Aikido dojo from Plymouth, UK that shows O'Sensei performing what appears to be a variation of kata gatame, or shoulder lock. Here is the link to that photo: **http://farm3.static.flickr.com/2088/2038285023_3db492ae15.jpg**

The following will describe kata gatame. Uke is lying on his back underneath O'Sensei who is positioned at about a 45-degree angle on top and leaning on the right side of uke. He is horizontal to the mat, with his upper body weight pushing down on uke, his hakama and the angle in which the photo was taken, makes it impossible to tell if O'Sensei's knees are touching the mat or if he is pushing his weight upon uke through his feet. This technique appears to be a blood choke, as

O'Sensei's right arm is tight around uke's neck applying a tight squeeze on the carotid artery. His bicep and/or shoulder also appear to be putting pressure on the trachea, making the technique a combination of a blood-choke and air-choke. Because O'Sensei's left fingers can be seen on the mat below uke's occipital region, he is probably grabbing his own left wrist with his right hand. This also puts pressure on the back of uke's neck. O'Sensei's right hand appears to be in the process of grabbing his left forearm. Uke attempts to relieve the pressure on his neck and push O'Sensei away by extending his right forearm into O'Sensei's throat. O'Sensei counters by turning his head to the left side, tucking his chin, and burying the side of his face into the empty space created by uke's left forearm. This process increases the pressure of the choke, protects O'Sensei's neck and face, and allows him to use gravity as well as his center for stabilization, whereas uke is only able to push using the strength of his arms. Uke is probably ready to tap with his left hand on the side of O'Sensei's left shoulder. This is a very good pin, neck-crank, and choke that stops the blood flow to the carotid artery as well as a strangulation that cuts off oxygen to the lungs by constricting the windpipe.

There is also another video on YouTube of Masatomi Ikeda (Japanese seventh dan aikido from Aikikai Hombu) performing newaza. (https://www.youtube.com/watch?v=85JxmlesOHk)

Some people perceive aikido only by the identification of technique and ignore O'Sensei's legacy and message. There is the assumption that if you do not perform the typical aikido techniques such as ikkyo, nikyo, kotegaeshi, shihonage, iriminage, etc., it is not true aikido. In this regard, if you perform the aforementioned techniques in conjunction with other nonconforming techniques, some believe that it is no longer authentic aikido. However, it is our belief that O'Sensei's conception of aikido was based on core principles that permeated all movement and strategies of defense rather than by a few limited basic techniques.

Other Japanese aikido instructors have been seen teaching newaza during aikido seminars. Some participants scratched their heads, wondering why this was the topic being taught, but did it anyway. Remember that since a martial arts master does not always include in his curriculum every technique he knows, that does not mean that those extra-curricular techniques are not part of the art.

Obviously, aikido's technical evolution has progressed from its initial version. This does not make modern aikido inferior or invalid. O'Sensei said that the techniques of today will be different tomorrow. The essence of aikido is its adaptability in both theory and practice. This is natural. Like flowing water, aikido never stagnates.

Here is a final example of the tradition versus adaptation discussion. One night during a regularly scheduled aikido class, a visitor entered Andrade-Shihan's dojo. Looking over the dojo, the visitor noticed a photograph of Andrade-Shihan performing a particular throw (ganseki-otoshi), otherwise known as "rock drop" throw. The visitor approached Andrade-Shihan and told him that the throw so pictured was inconsistent with traditional aikido principles.

Andrade-Shihan performing ganseki-otoshi   Andrade-Shihan performing ganseki-otoshi

Andrade-Shihan also demonstrates this technique dynamically both in the dojo and outdoors in his dvd "Mastering Your Mind With Aikido."

He explained his conception of traditional aikido in an attempt to discredit Andrade's aikido. Andrade-Shihan responded, "If you return, I have something to show you that may change your mind." Andrade-Shihan asked the visitor if he knew who Morihiro Saito was. He said he did and the visitor described Saito in depth, explaining how he was a traditional aikido practitioner and the person who studied the longest under O'Sensei. The visitor was intrigued enough to return to the dojo to see what he would be shown.

When he returned, the visitor was handed an aikido Journal Magazine (1996, vol. #23, no. 4) showing Morihiro Saito-Sensei on the front cover performing the very technique that he so adamantly protested as not being aikido. When the visitor compared the cover photograph with the photograph in the dojo, he was at a loss for words and could not respond to the contrary. Andrade-Shihan also had a book of Saito-Sensei (Traditional Aikido, vol. 4, p. 107) with a page of five photographs demonstrating the same technique. Andrade-Shihan then asked if he knew of Hiroshi Isoyama-Sensei. Isoyama-Sensei demonstrated a similar technique as Saito-Sensei in an Aiki expo demonstration video filmed in Japan. Finally, Andrade-Shihan showed the visitor a photograph of Isoyama-Sensei performing this same technique in an issue of Aikido Journal Magazine (2000, vol. 27, no. 1, p. 6).

Ganseki otoshi is not a common technique performed in aikido dojo, but because Saito-Sensei did it, the throw is now considered as an acceptable part of aikido's repertoire. If Saito-Sensei's performance of ganseki-otoshi made the throw "traditional," should not Morihei Ueshiba's performance of newaza make it traditional? If Saito is not sufficiently authoritative, Morihei Ueshiba's performance of the same technique is found in the book *Budo: Teachings of the Founder of Aikido*, page 127. Eliminate the double standard.

For those who may question the authenticity of the black and white book cover photo as truly being Morihei Ueshiba performing newaza, below is another different newaza submission of O'Sensei using the same uke. Notice Morihei Ueshiba's face, which adds a high degree of credibility to the evidence of his presence both in this photo and on the cover. In this photo, O'Sensei traps uke's entire right upper extremity away from uke's body to apply pain to the shoulder and elbow joints. Simultaneously, he leans forward in order to apply pain and pressure directly and firmly against uke's right side of the neck with his right forearm (ulnar bone) for a shimewaza (choking technique).

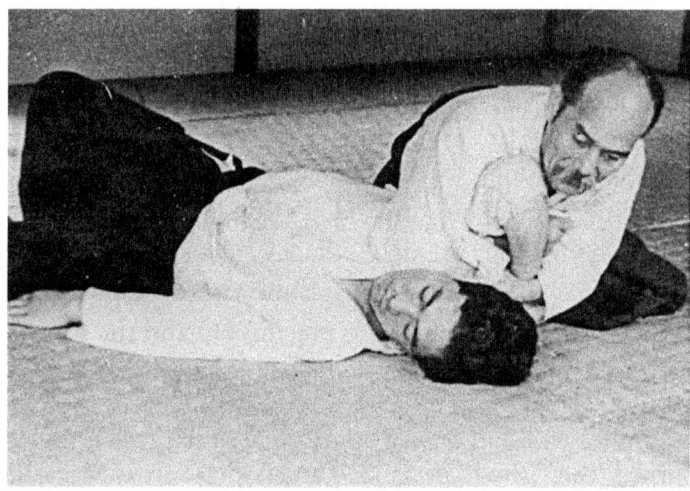

Mukei No Ryu aikido accepts the usefulness of newaza training for dealing with certain tactical situations. Newaza is also viewed as consistent with aikido's basic philosophy of taking an opponent to the ground when necessary and maintaining control through pain compliance. Including newaza into the formal curriculum will revive the tradition of newaza practice, ensuring that it will not be lost through complacency or ignorance. The only remaining relevant question is whether or not some forms of newaza (Mukei No Ryu Aiki-Newaza) are consistent with and utilize the basic principles of aikido.

Is It Jujutsu or Aikido?

There are literally thousands of different styles of martial arts in the world today. Some are of authentic old school lineage while others are fairly modern. Still, there are those that evolved from traditional martial arts while some are recent inventions that borrow eclectically from other styles. This is enough to make your head spin. So how does one tell the difference between one art and another when different arts can have the same techniques? For example, how does one discern an aikido technique from a jujutsu technique from observation without someone identifying them for you? Even more difficult is distinguishing between different styles within the same general art—a Yoshinkan Aikido technique from a Shin Shin Toitsu Aikido (formerly known as Ki Society) technique. Then, where do Mukei No Ryu aikido and its many variations of techniques fit?

To answer the above questions, we must first define what characterizes a few of these arts without examining every single martial art. These are, of course, generalizations with minor nuances from style to style but nevertheless, should provide a rudimentary understanding. As previously explained, many of the Japanese martial arts can be traced back to Koryu Bujutsu, old traditional martial arts that were used on the battlefield. These are most often schools of jujutsu and/or aikijujutsu. From these bujutsu evolved many different styles of gendai budo (modern martial systems) including, but not limited to, certain jujutsu, aikido, judo and so on. Sometimes these budo were developed to have a different purpose than bujutsu. Budo often incorporates spiritual endeavors that were of less concern to bujutsu practitioners. That is not to say that budo is ineffective or that bujutsu practitioners lacked any spirituality.

Let us compare Nihon jujutsu (founded by Shizuya Sato), a traditional koryu method, with aikido in order to better distinguish between the techniques of these two systems. According to the Nihon Jujutsu website http://nihonjujutsu.com/faq.php,

Jujutsu (also written jujitsu or jiu jitsu) is a Japanese martial art that is considered the mother art of aikido, and employs many of the same principles as aikido. Like the striking arts karate and kung-fu, jujutsu teaches the effective use of striking methods, as well as the use of vital points as targets for striking in self-defense. Jujutsu also incorporates weapons practice: the tanbo for self-defense, as well as defense against such weapons as the knife, pistol, and jo (staff). Nihon jujutsu contains techniques also found in a variety of martial arts such as aikido, bagua, hsingi, iaido, jujutsu, judo, kali, karate, kendo, kickboxing, kung fu, san chuan dao, taekwondo, and tai chi.

Aikido, as defined by the Aikikai website http://www.aikikai.or.jp/eng/, states that

Aikido movement maintains this firm and stable center with an emphasis on spherical rotation characterized by flowing, circular, dance-like motions. These pivoting, entering and circling motions are used to control and overcome the opponent. The principle of spherical rotation makes it possible to defend oneself from an opponent of superior size, strength, and experience. Although aikido movements are soft, rational, and smooth as in nature, by applying a bit of force, these can become devastatingly effective. The gentle quality of aikido makes it appealing to men and women and children regardless of age. It not only offers spiritual development but also provides exercise and teaches proper etiquette and behavior.

Morihei Ueshiba studied many styles of jujutsu, judo and most importantly, Daito-Ryu aikijujutsu. Aikido's founder drew techniques from many arts to create his esoteric art. However, the fact that aikido styles and techniques may look similar to jujutsu techniques does not mean that there are no differences. For example, in the art of jujutsu, techniques can be applied by uprooting an opponent, causing the person to lose balance and then taking the opportunity to execute a throw. In aikido, the techniques are applied by redirecting the opponent's attacking force in a circular fashion. This creates the off-balance necessary to successfully apply a takedown followed by a pin and submission. So even when a similar technique (such as a hip throw) is applied, practitioners of jujutsu or aikido execute the technique differently based on distinct principles.

This distinction of principles is best understood experientially. Even a skilled onlooker may have difficulty distinguishing the two arts. Aikijujutsu and aikido are even harder to distinguish because Ueshiba's earlier aikido was derived from aikijujutsu and had not yet evolved into the softer style of his later years.

In addition to throwing, jujutsu teaches striking certain areas of the body with fingers, hands, elbows, feet, knees, legs, and head. Many aikido systems have tended to downplay atemi with either empty hand or weapons. Some aikido schools do not teach atemiwaza at all. As you will learn, this is not the position of Mukei No Ryu aikido.

Another major difference between aikido and jujutsu lies in the art's philosophy and the intent of the practitioners. Aikido teaches us to value the preservation of life. Permanently injuring another person is a last resort, although no aikidoka is required to forgo effective and necessary self-defense. O'Sensei underwent a long process of shugyo (ascetic exercises) to create aikido. The ethical and spiritual values that he embraced were, however, sometimes imperfectly and incomprehensibly transmitted to his students. Any progress that his art makes should be consistent with aikido's inherent spiritual principles. Jujutsu seems to have a less forgiving mentality and is more concerned with martial technique and effectiveness. So where does Mukei No Ryu fall?

Mukei No Ryu aikido's advanced newaza is designed to deal with street-style attacks in a manner that will initially appear to be like jujutsu. A careful examination of the instructional techniques in this book and the corresponding dynamic real-world video techniques (DVD) will bring to light the aikido principles operating within what will seem at times to be traditional jujutsu ground techniques. These aikido principles will appear subtly, suddenly and change rapidly as the encounter progresses. As you watch, remember that it is the underlying flow of the movement and the feeling of non-resistance leading into the techniques that distinguish aikido.

Aikido has a unique martial evolution from jujutsu, aikijujutsu, the sword and other arts. Thus, glimpses of these arts in the execution of certain aikido techniques should come as no surprise. Just because there are only a few photos of O'Sensei available performing newaza does not mean that he did not consider newaza to be a part of aikido.

So, some may say that certain techniques of Mukei No Ryu aikido look like jujutsu while others will say they are clearly aikido. In truth, the techniques are formless. One's expression of aikido is what it needs to be at any given moment.

If you wish to weaken

The enemy's sword

Move first, fly in and cut!

Poetic Songs of the Way
Morihei Ueshiba
Aiki News No. 46 March, 15, 1982

Calling All Grapplers!

In the realm of martial arts, judo, jujutsu, wrestling and MMA practitioners are considered the top of the grappling and ground-fighting arena. They generally focus their training in newaza, so you may be asking, "What can aikido offer these grappling aficionados?"

If knowledge is power, then learning a new perspective will make them better grapplers. For this reason, if everyone is fighting with similar strategies then a different approach may give them further insight into combat and an advantage in how to defend against others with comparable training. In addition, there are many different wrist and finger locks, shoulder pins, arm bars, and joint-manipulation techniques like nikyo, sankyo, yonkyo, shihonage, kotegaeshi, etc. that are used in aikido but are not used in these other arts because they are bound by competitive rules that restrict the use of such techniques. Since Mukei No Ryu aikido is not limited by rules and is more focused on self-defense applications, the inclusion of this type of technique makes sense. In Mukei No Ryu aikido, there is also the use of strikes, which judo does not traditionally use. Consequently, there is an armamentarium of techniques that can be added to their arsenal.

If you pay attention to the current state of the UFC you will see proof of this because of one of aikido's most famous practitioners and action film star, Steven Segal-Shihan. Renowned fighters have approached Segal-Shihan after seeing the knockout results during Anderson Silva's fight against Vitor Belfort. In an interview, Silva credits Segal-Shihan with teaching him the kick that won him the fight. Another fighter, Lyoto Machida, also showed his respect to the actor for teaching him an equally impressive kick that knocked out Randy Couture. So, if aikido can help these professional fighters with their striking, why not their newaza? By the way, aikido generally does not teach defenses against kicks, but like Segal-Shihan, we do.

A calm mind can help in any fighting situation. The more focused and relaxed a person is, correlates to being able to perceive danger faster, react more efficiently and make better rational decisions. When a person can learn to reduce the stress from conflict, there is an increased likelihood for survival. Aikido can help with this too. Aikido teaches certain breathing methods that help relax the mind and body. These specialized breathing methods also help improve how a person respires. By controlling the breathing process, a person will have greater endurance and therefore be able to relax and endure without tiring as quickly.

Last but not least, because of aikido's system of teaching non-resistance, a grappler who learns it is likely to develop a greater sensitivity to movement. They will learn to yield and redirect an opponents force and use it to set up a defense. Confronting an attacker with muscle usually results with the stronger person winning; taking the energy of the opponent and using it allows a weaker person to prevail.

Getting the Most from Newaza Training

In order to get the most from newaza, you must have a balance in training between repetition of technique and spontaneous free-flowing practice. Correct repetition of a technique is essential for having a successful outcome in a physical confrontation. It is said that it takes more than ten thousand times of repeating a movement in order for the body to ingrain it into muscle memory. Again, it is better to have a few defenses executed repeatedly and mastered than many that you have done only on occasion. Remember, one of the main differences between a beginner and a master is the amount of time the master has spent in consistent study.

The many techniques that comprise a martial arts curriculum are designed to offer students various effective defenses against a myriad of confrontational situations. Aikido is known for its multitudinous variations amongst its techniques as a result of cultivating spontaneous movements. However, certain basic movements and techniques form a core foundation that one revisits during training to develop certain skill sets. Expert martial artists know that quality of technique, not quantity, makes the master. Get to know your techniques intimately and practice them frequently in all types of scenarios. This includes engaging your opponent in newaza from various attacks both standing and on the ground.

As you practice newaza, you must also have time to test your skills against a partner who is actively trying to counter, resist, and subdue you as well. Moreover, you must practice with people of varying body types, both large and small. This will develop speed, fluidity of movement and instinctive interactions among different defenses. In other words, this ongoing process cultivates adaptability. You may even begin to learn how to anticipate your opponent's actions. Newaza is a little like playing chess. Bold moves, feints, and sacrifices are all part of the action. But, before you get to this stage, you must place yourself on the game board by displaying something as simple as correct posture and the proper mindset.

You must realize this!

Aiki cannot be captured with the brush

Nor can it be expressed with the mouth

And so it is that one must proceed

to realization (satori).

Poetic Songs of the Way
Morihei Ueshiba (1883-1969)
Aiki News No. 46 March, 15, 1982

Mukei No Ryu Aikido:
An Overview

Mukei No Ryu is the style of aikido developed and taught by Andrade-Shihan at the Aikido Tenshinkai of Florida dojo in Orlando, Florida. Mukei No Ryu aikido distills over fifty years of experience in a variety of unarmed and weapons-based martial arts into a practical self-defense system that remains firmly grounded in traditional aikido principles. The name Mukei No Ryu originated during the Kokusai Budoin/IMAF fiftieth anniversary commemorative special event held in Japan, in March 2002. At this event, Andrade-Shihan performed aikido demonstrations as part of the celebration of the twenty sixth All Japan Budo Exhibition held at Hibiya Park in Tokyo.

Following the many different aikido demonstrations at the event, Andrade-Shihan was approached by many renowned budoka, including many aikidoka, from the United States of America, Japan and Europe. They all inquired as to what style he had demonstrated. Andrade-Shihan said, "It is my own natural style." The budoka saw it as a truly different aikido style, unlike any they had seen before. Japanese aikidoka called it Mukei No Ryu, which translates as "style transcending form." To this day, martial artists, including aikidoka, express curiosity about his style. It just does not fit any of the other known aikido systems they have seen.

Mukei No Ryu aikido is a highly eclectic, improvisational system of aikido. Since no single martial art is totally effective against all attacks under all conditions, Mukei No Ryu aikido uses an arsenal of defenses that can include any physical activity and martial technique. Whichever technique is chosen will be performed in accordance with the basic principles of aikido. This allows a union of traditional aikido with contemporary needs and sensibilities to form a highly effective method of self-defense and a graceful and powerful art.

Aikido is typically characterized as a defensive martial art. However, many practitioners often misinterpret this to mean that aikidoka should passively wait and respond only to physical attacks (e.g. strikes and grabs) once they have been initiated. According to Mukei No Ryu principles this is incorrect. For any martial art to be viable in a self-defense situation, it is important that the practitioner be alert of the surroundings and if a physical confrontation becomes inevitable, to respond effectively to the attacker's intent rather than waiting for the attacker's action. The appropriate response may in fact begin with a pre-emptive atemi once the attacker has violated the aikidoka's personal space with intent to harm. In other words, a defensive martial art instructs us to avoid unprovoked assaults, but does shackle us from acting first, when this would end the encounter and enable escape.

This aikido upholds and is true to O'Sensei's ideals and principles of aikido. Healing is preferable to destruction; however, one cannot speak and act effectively from a position of weakness. As such, students of Mukei No Ryu aikido train with a pragmatic mentality. Even so, a noncompetitive environment allows students from different martial backgrounds, evincing smiles, to explore energy interactions as both uke and nage. Practice partners engage in training that evokes personal development, both outer and inner, as the ethical implications inherent in aikido techniques become clear through years of consistent training. Advanced students are afforded opportunities to experience takemusu aiki and Zen-like enlightenment. These students will make the art of aikido their own. They will preserve its integrity and bring their unique talents and predilections into the creative process of individuation.

The technical aspects of aikido have changed over time. The art is different from that taught and practiced by Morihei Ueshiba. Techniques change as society and people change. Even Ueshiba's execution of techniques changed over his lifetime. Mukei No Ryu aikido is not about remaking or transforming Ueshiba's fundamental principles, philosophy, values, or message; rather, it carries on all traditions as well as expounding upon aikido's essential elements. It focuses on aikido's roots in traditional Japanese jujutsu and kenjutsu (The Samurai's way of the sword). It embraces change and celebrates other martial arts, including the different styles of aikido and their individual paths of development—all are welcome in the aikido family.

So, how is Mukei No Ryu aikido similar to and different from the various styles that evolved from O'Sensei's martial art? Here follow eleven characteristics of Mukei No Ryu aikido as taught by Andrade-Shihan in his Orlando dojo, Nemeroff-Shihan in his Whitehall, Pennsylvania dojo and other instructors of the Mukei No Ryu lineage.

1. Mukei No Ryu aikido adheres to the following five fundamental principles of aikido theory and practice: **Keep One Point** by focusing consciousness in your center, the one point in the lower abdomen just below the navel, throughout the application of a technique. **Move from the center** by leading from the one point from which your power flows. **Turn when pushed, enter when pulled** to negate resistance to someone's attack. By doing so, the attacker becomes unbalanced. **Keep weight underside** by relaxing upper muscles and using lower muscles. As examples, relax the upper body while maintaining a heavy and stable feeling from the hips downward. Relax the bicep arm muscle and use the arm's tricep muscle to achieve a condition called "unbendable arm." **Extend ki** by following through while executing a technique, punch, kick or an evasive redirecting movement. Power should not be blocked or restricted in any way. Utilize proper

breathing to move ki through and around the body.

2. Mukei No Ryu aikido embraces all types of martial technique, including but not limited to, empty-hands (immobilizations and throws), ground grappling (mount, guard and so on) weapons (bokken, jo, knife, tanbo, hanbo, and others), striking (punches and kicks), submissions (chokes, pins, arm bars, and pressure point applications), discretionary disengagement (avoiding confrontation), and any other available tools to end a physical confrontation in your favor. In this spirit, we are fervently trying to fill the knowledge void.

3. There is an understanding that anything and everything is acceptable to use in the pursuit of self-protection. There are no limits to using makeshift weapons found in the surrounding environment. Likewise, there are no limits on using any technique that is applied in accordance with aikido's energetic principles.

4. Mukei No Ryu aikido teaches the liberal use of atemi. This is not the case with some other aikido styles. When an attacker is noncompliant, a strike may be needed in order to prevent further resistance. A strike, or even the threat of a strike, can create movement in a person who is rooted and unwilling to move. Sometimes, a strike to certain areas of the body can reignite the aiki process of movement. Atemi to various precise and specific vital areas of the body may be the first and only defensive move to deprive an attacker's offensive actions and determine the outcome of a violent altercation. One can atemi rapidly and with intent to any part of the body.

   Some aikido schools totally refrain from atemiwaza while others only limit atemi to the use of open handed strikes like tegatana (sword hand), shomenuchi (top of the head strike), yokomenuchi (side of the head strike), and munetsuki (breast bone chest thrust) attacks. We use these plus any other conceivable strikes. In fact, almost every body part can be used to deliver an atemi.

5. Mukei No Ryu aikido embraces suwariwaza as a form of newaza. Whereas some aikido schools limit newaza to suwariwaza, Mukei No Ryu aikido uses suwariwaza as a point of departure for further exploration of grappling. Thus, newaza can be performed starting from tachiwaza, hanmi handachiwaza, suwariwaza or any other position. Basically, intent, strategy, and tactics are the same regardless in which position one finds oneself.

6. This system upholds O'Sensei's desire for peace and his unwillingness to cause more harm than is necessary in the pursuit of self-defense. However, Mukei No Ryu aikido does not subscribe to the pacifist philosophy of nonviolence that prohibits defense of self and others. It is, first and foremost, pragmatic with deep spiritual undertones.

7. Mukei No Ryu aikido embraces a balanced and harmonious relationship between self-defense, personal spiritual growth, and overall wellness. Since a martial school that only teaches theory without practical combat training ceases to be a martial art, practical self-defense practice, including training in newaza, is essential for a student to transcend his or her self-imposed limits. From a spiritual perspective, performing techniques from a strong, stable center, maintaining correct posture, and moving circularly relaxes the body, focuses the mind and generates ki, or power. Strong, free-flowing ki enhances the student's wellness and contributes to his or her ability to thrive during long-term training.

8. Mukei No Ryu aikido offers kyu (ranks below black belt) members a structure of set techniques, a testing system based on students' readiness to perform, belts to display progress, and a systematized methodology of practice involving various levels of resistance. This is only the beginning. Once a student learns the basic techniques, things start to change. As the students' abilities evolve, numerous variations on basic techniques are presented. At some point in students' training, techniques will begin to emerge spontaneously from evasive movement. Students have the opportunity to display takemusu aiki during randori (defense against multiple attackers) training. Under the psychological pressure cooker of being attacked by up to five people at once, a student's body-mind may take over and demonstrate remarkable feats of evasion, self-defense, and the body. Similar movements of the body-mind can occur during one-on-one newaza practice.

9. Mukei No Ryu aikido also employs a very unique approach to imparting its methods to an aikidoka. The teaching is directed at the student's body-mind through the fatiguing of his or her conscious mind. This pedagogical technique produces a spontaneous emergence of technique by helping the student to let go of unnecessary thinking. This result is achieved, in part, by frequently changing the training and not allowing the aikidoka to dwell on any one technique for too long at one time. This method tires the rational mind and allows it to relax and become pliable. Under these circumstances, one's sense of self subsides and so clears the way for the body and its ki to function without hindrance (a state known as mushin, or no-mindedness). This is the foundational state of consciousness from which all takemusu aiki emerges.

10. Mukei No Ryu aikido students aim to understand the complete scope of the art. As a comprehensive martial art, aikido is adaptable as part of its very nature; therefore, its practitioners are also adaptable to changing situations. The incorporation of newaza into aikido as a kind of aiki-newaza is one example of the art's ability to apply its principles to other techniques and exemplify them.

11. Like most other schools of aikido, Mukei No Ryu aikido prohibits competition. This also applies to newaza training. Ethically, one should not be rewarded with a prize for injuring another person and a student's focus should always be on self-cultivation instead of a trophy or medal. Students train to learn the ground techniques and gradually respond with fluid movement and instant awareness. That is the reward. Students are instructed to tap out immediately when a painful technique is applied. The goal is to teach students how to defend themselves on the ground practically without ego becoming involved. This ensures good relations between training partners and may save one's life on the street.

Even more than the above-mentioned distinctions, there is something about Mukei No Ryu aikido that must be experienced for it to be understood. Like trying to describe the taste of a sweet mango to someone who has never tasted one, you must try Mukei No Ryu to grasp its flavor. We invite you to take a bite.

Put the active principle (yo) into the right hand

Turn the left hand into passive (in)

And so guide the adversary.

> Poetic Songs of the Way
> Morihei Ueshiba (1883-1969)
> Aiki News No. 46 March, 15, 1982

Fundamental Aikido Techniques

As stated in the Introduction, we felt it necessary to include some core aikido techniques typically done as a standing defense. Why would we put these in a book about newaza, you may ask? The reason is simply because by being able to visualize the techniques from a standing position, it is easier to understand how these are performed on the ground. Newaza techniques are a reflection of tachiwaza.

Seven such techniques are illustrated and briefly described below.

Ikkyo

Ikkyo is often called the first principle technique of aikido. Essentially, application of this technique brings the attacker to the ground, resting on his stomach. Pinning the attacker to the ground and submitting him is accomplished by applying pressure to the proximal edge of the elbow near the ulnar nerve.

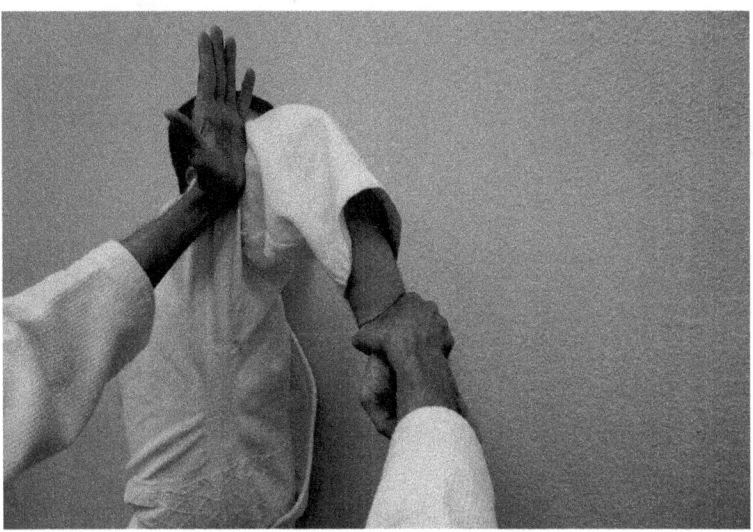

Following uke's strike, nage immobilizes the arm by firmly gripping the wrist and raising the elbow in a circular upward fashion toward the attacker's head.

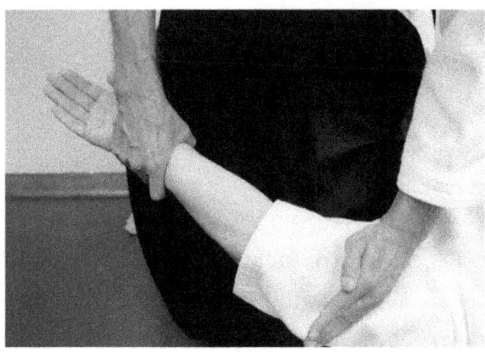 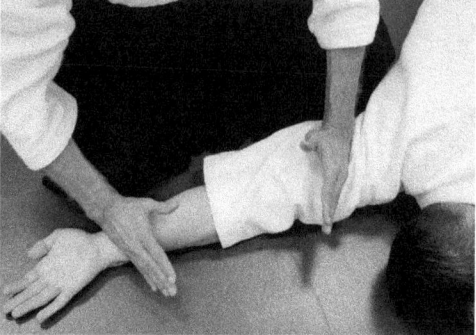

After nage applies circular downward pressure to the arm and shoulder to bring uke to the ground, face down; nage sits seiza alongside uke wedging his knee into uke's armpit for leverage and control. Nage finishes with the pin described above.

Nikyo

Nikyo is known as the second principle of aikido. Application of this technique causes great pain to the wrist and has the potential to damage the wrist, ligaments and tendons. Nikyo is applied by simultaneously compressing and rotating the wrist. At the same time, uke's elbow is pulled inward to assist in the compression of the wrist.

Illustrated below are two versions of nikyo. The first technique counters grabbing of one's shoulder or lapel (kata-dori). The other counters a cross wrist grab (kosa-dori).

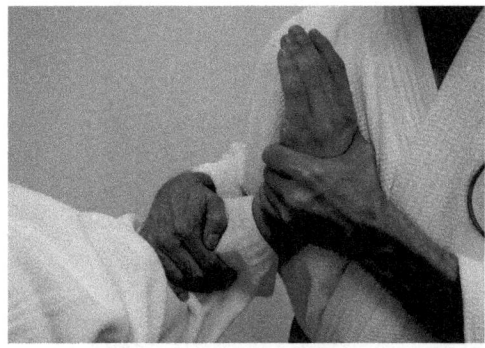 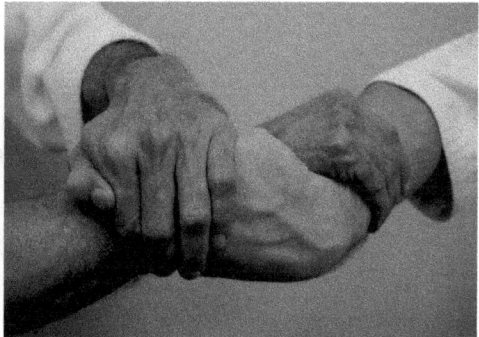

Sankyo

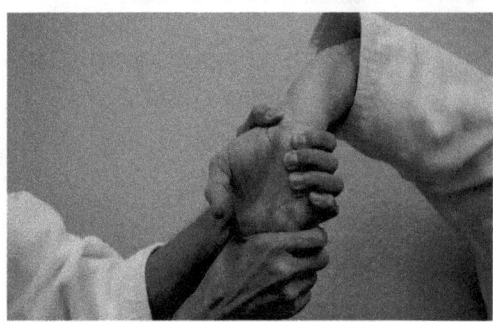

Sankyo, or the third principle also causes great pain to the wrist. There is a vertical alignment of the hand, wrist and elbow with the elbow positioned slightly forward from the hand. The fingers are pointing downward toward the ground. Once this position is secured, a medial rotation of the wrist causes the pain.

Yonkyo

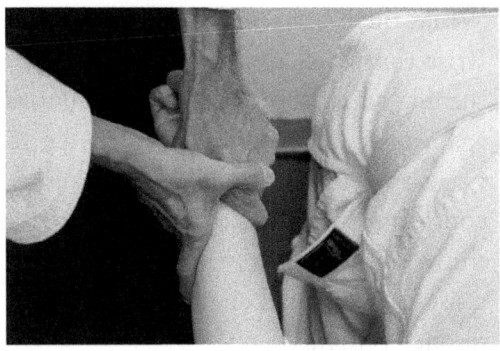

The fourth principle of aikido is somewhat similar to sankyo. Yonkyo also uses a vertical alignment of the hand, wrist, and elbow. However, pain is inflicted by a downward and "wringing out" motion of the distal forearm with the second metacarpal phalangeal joints. Similar to the way a bokken is grabbed, pressure is applied simultaneously along the radial and ulnar nerves distally.

Gokyo

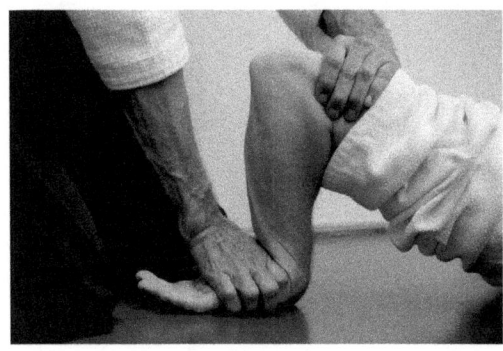

Gokyo is the fifth principle. After uke has been taken to the ground and lays prone, his wrist is placed directly under his elbow such that the arm, elbow and hand are similar in appearance to the letter Z. However, both the elbow and wrist are flexed to form a ninety degree angle with uke's palm facing upward. Then, downward pressure is applied to the elbow so that the wrist is compressed while being simultaneously rotated. This forms a formidable ground submission.

Shihonage

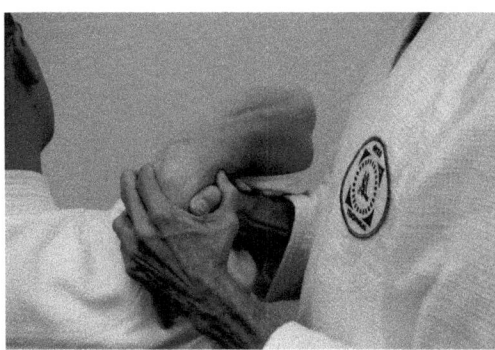

The "four corner throw" takedown technique sends uke reeling downward to the ground. Leverage is achieved by a flexion and torsion to the wrist and elbow that locks both. Note that nage's center is facing uke's center. Care should be taken when practicing this technique as it can damage the wrist, elbow and shoulder.

Kotegaeshi

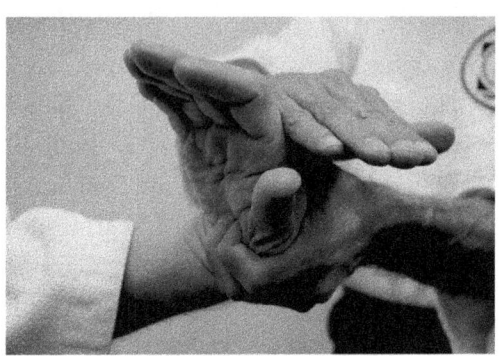

While there are several versions of this wrist throw, all of them throw uke by turning his wrist outward and downward against the natural flexion of the wrist. Nage can use the hand blade to reinforce control and pressure to uke's wrist. This throw is more effective when the wrist twist forms a small circle placed in front of one's center.

Strategic Insights of Mukei No Ryu Aikido

Morihei Ueshiba once said, "It is necessary to develop a strategy that utilizes all the physical conditions and elements that are directly at hand. The best strategy relies upon an unlimited set of responses." For the modern aikidoka, newaza refined from the strategies and tactics of ancient budo can be an essential and practical response to any confrontations. While exponents of Mukei No Ryu aikido aim to avoid confrontations, if there is no other choice but to engage in a violent altercation, an aikidoka must use whatever is necessary to subdue the attacker. Keep in mind that there are ethical and legal ramifications to any violent confrontation. The aikidoka should not be the initial aggressor; and even if not, the aikidoka may still incur a civil lawsuit. Review your state's self-defense laws, including any "stand your ground" law.

When an aikidoka applies certain techniques, the pain produced in the attacker's joints and ligaments should be enough to control the attacker and cause submission. When pain-producing techniques are taken to extremes, they can cause irreversible damage. The ethical intent of the aikidoka is not to reach these extremes unless it is absolutely necessary for survival.

The philosophy and principles of Mukei No Ryu aikido apply equally whether one is standing or on the ground. On the ground, the dynamics of a volatile situation can change quickly, so techniques should manifest spontaneously once the aikidoka receives the energy of an attack. As an aikidoka gets more tangled up and range of movement becomes ever more restricted, it is essential to relax and employ a non-resisting aiki strategy against oncoming attacks. Also, an aikidoka should not act with tunnel vision, focusing narrowly on one certain technique. Pre-planning a response without knowing the kind of attack coming may cause the aikidoka to miss the opportunity to perform a more effective technique that is better suited for the situation presented.

Some martial artists intentionally go to the ground and lie on their backs in order to bring the fight down to them where they will attempt to defend from that position. During a fight, a goal of Mukei No Ryu aikido is to remain standing. If on the ground, attempt to return to a standing position as soon as possible. Also, if another attacker shows up to help the first, the aikidoka must return to a standing position as quickly as possible or risk facing injury or death. During the transition to a standing position, the attacker on top will certainly attempt to strike, choke, restrain and/or apply a joint lock. Be prepared!

Spend time practicing defenses from all positions, including standing, different grapples and holds on the ground. Having only one or two practice partners limits an aikidoka's growth and fosters stagnation, so It is helpful to train with multiple people of all sizes and skill levels. By doing so, the aikidoka will be better equipped to defend against all types of assailants. People having different body types will have to adjust their newaza strategies and tactics to accommodate their physiques. For example, someone having longer arms and legs will have different approaches and choose different techniques than someone with shorter extremities.

An aikidoka engaged in newaza should stay close and connected to the attacker. The best technicians often close all the gaps and eliminate spaces where applicable (constriction will be explained in more detail subsequently). Doing so helps prevent opening oneself up for a reversal and/or a counter attack by an assailant and provides added protection against retaliatory strikes. In most situations, keeping one's limbs close to the body is also essential because the farther away from the body they are, the more vulnerable they become to attack. A skilled practitioner often waits for the opponent to extend an arm and/or leg in order to take advantage and apply a finishing technique.

Being exposed in the prone position, or laying flat, face down, is extremely dangerous. This is potentially one of the worst positions to defend from the ground. The attacker can strike at will against an unprotected head, neck and torso. The only defense available is tucking in the chin to avoid a choke and using one's hands to cover the back of the head and neck. If at all possible, the aikidoka, not assuming that any effective defense is possible from this position, must promptly change to the supine and ultimately to the standing position. Exposure in the prone position is a common and unfortunate mistake in newaza made by beginner and advanced practitiioners alike. This tactical blunder usually results from inexperience, lack of stamina, loss of concentration and the inability to focus. It is difficult and almost impossible to defend yourself and survive incoming attacks if you remain in the prone position. In many dojo, students comply with the technique without ever feeling the realism of resistance. Training beyond this point stops and fails to fulfill the real significance of martial arts as a means of self-defense. One is left with only an illusion of safety. Interestingly, the majority of participants are aware of this fact, criticize the art, but do nothing to change it. If you do not advance beyond this point, you are not going to foster the necessary perceptual and reactive speed or skill to thwart an attack of this nature.

In martial arts training, as in living daily life, a wise person examines and evaluates both triumphs and failures in order to learn from successes and avoid repeating mistakes. The more newaza is practiced, deconstructed and analyzed, the more quickly these skills can be perfected. If an aikido school has access to video equipment then newaza sessions can be recorded and analyzed much like NFL team players watch video of their own and their opponents' performances.

To see the true things

Harmonize with the voice which shouts,

"Yah!"

Never be drawn into the rhythm of the enemy.

Poetic Songs of the Way
Morihei Ueshiba (1883-1969)
Aiki News No. 46 March, 15, 1982

THE CLINCH:
A LIKELY TRANSITION FROM TACHIWAZA TO NEWAZA

When a fight lasts more than a few minutes, it is quite likely that the combatants may transition into a close-range grappling scenario known as the clinch. The clinch establishes the first initial tactile connection as uke and nage start to grapple at close quarters in front, behind or side of each other. Classical examples of standard traditional aikido clinch include techniques such as the choke from the rear (ushiro kubi shime) and grabbing both shoulders from the front (ryokata dori). These, as well as other clinch holds, should be practiced while keeping one's center, maintaining a proper distance, and all other fundamental principles of aikido. Below are some photographic examples of various clinches.

Traditional aikido clinch known as ryokata dori

Traditional aikido clinch known as ushiro kubi shime

Shoulder to shoulder clinch

Double underhooks clinch

Rear bodylock clinch

The rear clinch is considered the most advantageous position because it is difficult to defend. The objective of the clinch is to tie, restrict, and control the movements of the other person, deliver close strikes with the head, fists, elbows, knees, and feet, to rest and create a pause when fatigued, or to sweep one or both legs to break balance in order to provide an effective takedown or to execute a throw. The nature of the clinch often occurs in matches during competitive martial sports with participants in judo, sanbo, muay thai, mixed martial arts, wrestling, wing chun, boxing, etc. In some competitive martial sports, clinching is not allowed if it goes for too long. In which case, the combatants would be issued a warning from the referee.

Although it is likely for uke to initiate the attack, it is nage's strategy to make the initial contact by responding quickly, effectively, and efficiently after evading the attack in preparation for defensive movements. In other words, as soon as one perceives the attacker lunging and attempting a grab, is the time when one begins the process of intercepting and redirecting the attack to off-balance uke. In aikido, it is fundamental not to meet the opponent's force with force or to lose balance if overextended, but to blend and redirect the force of the attack with an unobstructed empty mind. Rotating the hips and pelvis with fluid and fast turning movements are also crucial for proper body control in preparation for the anticipation of the opponent's movements.

During the dynamics of the clinch, proper and timely, synchronized and relaxed rhythms of displacing the body should be used. By gliding the feet across the ground and not having a very wide or very narrow separation between the feet while maintaining the knees slightly bent, allows for a more favorable displacement in any several strategic positions. This more likely causes nage's balance to be properly maintained while trying to execute the next phase of grappling.

For maximum results, once the clinch has been established, it is important for the aikidoka to avoid looking down at the forward, backward, or side movements of each other's feet or become preoccupied at the way he has been grabbed. Nage should visualize with soft eyes, i.e. with a wide field of view, and not focused on any particular place or person. Looking down is a sure way to miss a potential incoming strike. It is not a good idea to grab clothes because of the flimsiness of the fabric; instead one should grab body parts directly.

The clinch is a transitional period of combat that can evolve into different scenarios depending on the dynamics of the situation. The person may escape, and remain standing to move freely again or progress to the next phase of grappling, newaza. If you engage in the clinch and find yourself being taken to the floor, attempt to end up in one of the primary ground positions designed for effective submission. Ideally, nage should settle in one of these positions by the time he reaches the ground, and not wait until he gets there to begin applying a technique.

As stated earlier, in the many faces of the clinch, it is often inevitable that nage is unable to blend with uke's attack and execute a technique before uke is able to lunge in and gain a strong hold. It should not be the intended goal to end up in this position as it restricts movement and can ultimately lead to being wrestled to the ground. In this regard, do not neglect training in the many forms of the clinch, because you may have a false sense of security that you will not be caught there. Allow your training partner to grab you in many different ways, both in the traditional positions and beyond.

Work on becoming proficient in how to draw uke in different directions while he is attempting to grapple with you. Learn how to off-balance uke, and how to escape before a hold is on too tight to get away. Also train to avoid various strikes and holds such as painful uppercuts, the double collar tie, or two hands around the neck, and hits to the face or midsection with the knees from the clinch. Eventually, learn to execute all attacks and defenses with realism and resistance. Uke should attempt a more forceful attack on an advanced aikidoka by actually trying to grab, restrain, and pull nage off-balance and force him down. In the streets, rarely do things go as planned. The following photos depict a defense from the clinch.

Uke and nage face each other standing. Uke uses pressed elbows and his hands to grip around nage's back of the neck to apply a double collar tie clinch. This is a very effective way to control nage.

Nage's head is pushed down while maintaining the double collar tie. Uke delivers a right knee strike to nage's face. Nage begins to separate from uke, evades the knee strike by lowering his center, deflecting the attack with his left hand and lifting uke's left elbow with his right palm. It all occurs simultaneously.

Nage rises and escapes to a safe perpendicular positon very close to uke. Nage keeps his head tight behind uke's left shoulder. At the same time, nage maintains a tight grip with two hands at the level of the right arm distally, locking and trapping the upper extremities and restricting movements.

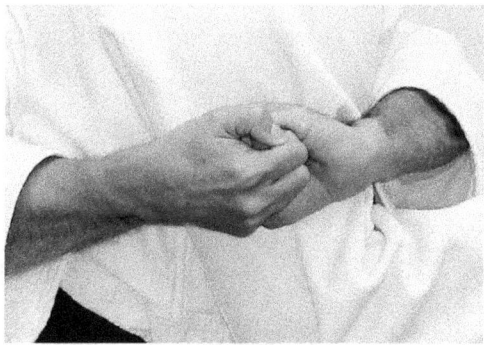

Pay close attention to the two hooks lock. In this case, it is best to lock the fingers underneath the fingers of the opposite hand and not entwine all ten fingers together.

Nage performs a quick rear naked choke. Note nage's dominant position as he also separates himself from uke to form a space that facilitates the creation of kuzushi to avoid retaliation by uke. For best results, as nage applies this technique, he shakes uke's neck using his upper extremities to tighten and to accomdate the choke. The above action is similar to the slithering movement of a snake.

Many examples of the clinch are demonstrated in the DVD and explained in detail in the Takin' It to the Street chapter which is full of comprehensive practical instructions and a helpful training guide.

Remember that it is very likely that if you lose your balance in the clinch, you may be taken to the ground. Which brings us to the next chapter about Kuzushi.

Though only one enemy calls you out

Be on your best guard

To deal with one adversary in the

spirit of facing ten thousands

Is the Way of the Warrior.

> Poetic Songs of the Way
> Morihei Ueshiba (1883-1969)
> Aiki News No. 46 March, 15, 1982

MASTERING KUZUSHI:
THE ART OF BREAKING BALANCE

Attacking with misdirected force and uncontrolled rage without a proper strategy is generally a useless waste of time and energy. Contrary to the belief that using brute strength is always the best strategy, moving subtly so as to off-balance the attacker can be a more effective approach. Only in such a way does a smaller person have a chance to control, subdue and defend against a larger attacker. This is the idea behind kuzushi.

Kuzushi is the art of altering the balance of your opponent to your advantage. In fact, it can be considered an art unto itself. Many great martial arts masters like Morihei Ueshiba and Jigoro Kano used this principle with great effect to develop the martial applications of their created arts. Perfection of this principle is not easy to achieve, but is an invaluable asset to any self-defense system.

Generally, in a fight, the first contact between the attacker and defender sets the tone for action. This is when kuzushi begins. While an aikidoka waits patiently for the attacker to initiate the first move, it is strategically the defender who anticipates the initial contact. This does not mean that the aikidoka becomes the aggressor; rather, he or she evades the attacker's force, connects with it while it is still in motion, and then redirects the energy. This strategy can off-balance the attacker, thereby setting up the use of a proper technique. We understand how difficult it is to express and to grasp aikido principles to a person who has no real familiarity or practice in aikido. It is like reading a book on how to sail without actual hands on experience.

In order to successfully execute a throw, submission or takedown, the attacker must be taken off-balance in some manner. Without the use of kuzushi by the defender, the attacker will most likely resist a technique and root into a stable posture. Grappling with such a person will feel like fighting a brick wall. Thus, the importance of kuzushi is obvious. By redirecting an attack during an altercation, which in and of itself may off-balance the attacker, far less effort needs to be exerted to successfully resolve the encounter in your favor. When proper kuzushi is applied, it should feel like uke is not there at all.

In aikido, kuzushi further relates directly to the application of non-resistance. For example, when being pulled, go with the flow and enter. When pushed, turn and yield to the principle of inertia (things in motion tend to stay in motion unless affected by an outside force). Using kuzushi uproots a stable attacker and allows an aikidoka to apply a technique. Thus, utilizing the principles of aiki and kuzushi make for a formidable self-defense strategy.

A person who strongly applies force in one direction can become anatomically weaker in other ways. To explain this, there is a rule of muscular physiology that states that typically muscles only contract in one direction, and two opposing muscles cannot contract at the same time. So, instead of moving directly against an attack where the muscles are strong, a person should move in a circular fashion to a safer position and apply a technique where the muscles are weaker. In this fashion, disrupting a person's posture and stability via kuzushi can make the attacker vulnerable. Without two forces opposing each other, the attacker becomes overextended. As a result, the defender's energy works in unison with that of the attacker in such a way that the attacker ultimately self-defeats.

Keep in mind that a strike can also cause kuzushi. How and where a strike is delivered affects the way a person reacts, leans and or falls. Intentional strikes to certain areas of the body can also manifest postural imbalances, which are integral to set up a throw and/or a favorable counter attack. For example, striking the stomach often causes a person to bend forward. Striking the face often causes a person to go backward.

Kuzushi can also be applied through the use of what we call a spiritual atemi, or striking the spirit. Sometimes no contact is needed at all in order for a person to become off-balanced. The use of a ki-ai (spirit yell), which is essentially a loud scream meant to startle an attacker is one example of this. A spiritual atemi can also be used in other ways to change a thought or action. One day in his youth, Nemeroff-Shihan was visiting a friend and driving through New Jersey. On the way there, he noticed a police officer behind him and turned down another street to avoid getting a ticket. Unfortunately, the officer followed him and eventually pulled him over. As he approached Nemeroff-Shihan's car, he had one hand on his flashlight and the other one on his gun. He looked anxious. Nemeroff knew this was a good opportunity to apply a spiritual atemi. When the officer knocked on the window and asked him why he turned down the side street, he replied, "Do you know where Route 21 is?" The officer literally took a step back, looked confused for a second, and then a funny thing happened. He took out his radio, called into dispatch and asked for directions. His facial expression changed, his anxiety level dropped visibly and he went from an aggressive posture to a peaceful one. After sharing the directions, he agreed to let Nemeroff-Shihan off with a warning. Although we are not saying to use this concept against police officers, it exemplifies an everyday use of how a spiritual atemi can create kuzushi.

Like tachiwaza, during newaza it is also essential to redirect the flow of the attacker's energy without trying to force any action intentionally. This is one distinction between aikido newaza and other arts where practitioners try to over power their opponent forcefully. Perfect timing is crucial in adapting to the ebb and flow of any kind of combat. Be willing to wait for an opportune time to move and engage the attacker or risk being subdued. As the attacker transitions from one movement to another, a proficient aikidoka can gain an advantage and even control the situation. Trying to prematurely initiate a grappling technique allows the attacker a chance to pull away. If pushed, the attacker will most likely resist and push back. It is more efficient to blend with the energy of the attack and flow harmoniously with the ever-changing tides of combat.

While on the ground, allow the opponent to commit to an attack and think he or she is in control. Then yield to the movement and redirect the attack. Take the attacker's inertia to the side to off-balance him or her. If you are in the supine position, use this opportunity to get the attacker off you so that you may return to a standing position. If you are on top, then use this opportunity to stabilize the opponent and finish with a technique.

Any uneven distribution of weight can result in getting thrown from the mount position. Leaning too hard in an attempt to resist a countermovement or to force the opponent into a submission may cause the person on top to become unstable.

The person in the mount position loses his balance after the person in the supine position elevates his hips and uses his hands simultaneously to escape.

Using feints and leads are other ways of creating distractions that off-balance an opponent. Feints and leads can change a person's way of thinking, his motivation and make an opponent react and over-commit leaving the person off-balanced and set up for a technique. During this process, a person's body will often react with a flinch or a gag-reflex type of jerking motion in order to compensate for what the person perceives to be an opening in the defender's position.

The following example should clarify. Nage is in the mount position and after several attempted strikes to uke's face, uke grabs nage's wrist to stop that attack. As a result, nage uses this opportunity of uke's overextended upper extremity to apply a reversal technique such as a cross-body, straight-arm lock (juji gatame) to immobilize and control uke.

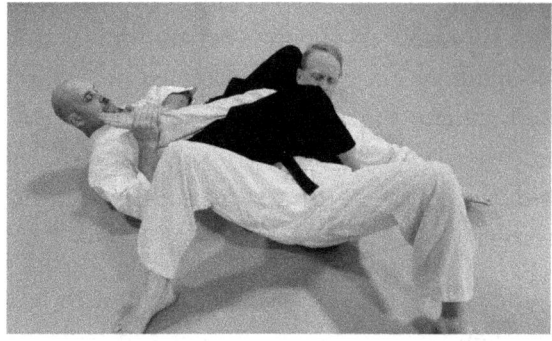

Nage executes a juji gatame

In general, when people discuss issues about kuzushi, it involves breaking the opponents balance. In order to accomplish this task, it is essential for the person attempting to perform kuzushi to keep his own balance intact. Imagine a spinning top that gets tapped and sent off its central axis. The result is that it spins haphazardly, out of control. This is a core principle that must be cultivated in the martial arts, especially aikido. If nage cannot remain stable, how is he expected to apply kuzushi to others? The following exercises culminate maintaining one's equilibrium during any martial activities.

The person on the bottom appears in the fetal position providing a stable platform. The person on top performs a series of sit-ups. This exercise is of tremendous benefit for any person who desires to maintain a stable center and excellent balance.

Clasp your hands behind your head and raise your head up slightly.

Begin a "bicycling" motion with your legs as each leg is extended and retracted in turn. When you have completed a desired number of repetitions, stop and carefully dismount your helper. After completing the dismount, your helper may rise up.

Whether the application of kuzushi is physical during combat or spiritual during every day events, its proper use can help defuse a volatile situation and turn it around in your favor. This concept is a key component to understanding almost every aspect of the martial arts and life.

The enemy comes running in to strike

At the instant of the attack

Avoid his strike with one step

And counter attack in that instant.

> Poetic Songs of the Way
> Morihei Ueshiba (1883-1969)
> Aiki News No. 46 March, 15, 1982

Exploring Aikido Principles with The Sangen

O'Sensei often described aikido self-defense strategies and tactics through the symbolic representation known as the sangen. The sangen is a multi-dimensional representation of the interactions of nature with humankind and, in like manner, interactions between two individuals during various phases of combat. The sangen uses three fundamental geometric figures (triangle, square and circle and their three-dimensional forms of pyramid, cube, and sphere) to represent the unity of mind, body, and spirit. This unification of mind, body, and spirit is at the heart of aikido's philosophy of resolving verbal and/or physical conflict and aggression in a nonresistant, noncompetitive, and nonviolent spiritual approach. This exploration of the sangen will proceed in the order of triangle, circle, and square as this best represents the order of these factors in a combat situation.

Triangle

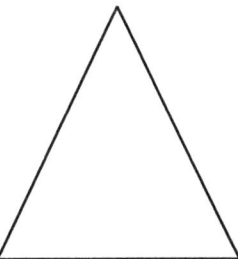

The triangle represents Irimi, or entering diagonally, not confrontational. Irimi is how one approaches a potential conflict. It also includes disengaging from conflict if at all possible. The triangle corresponds to the aikido ready stance. The triangular placement of one's feet forms a stable pyramidal stance from which to initiate any action. The triangle represents understanding the source of ki, or life force, generated during an encounter between opposing forces.

The following photos represent entering into a triangular position after an attack.

Nage enters to the rear (ura). His center faces uke at an oblique angle and off the line of attack. Note that nage's left foot is outside uke's right foot.

Nage enters to the front (omote). His center faces uke at an oblique angle and off the line of attack.

As it pertains to newaza, the triangle is demonstrated in various chokes using the upper and lower extremities. The triangle is also reflective of the dominant position of the mount, where nage positions himself on top of his opponent striking angularly downward.

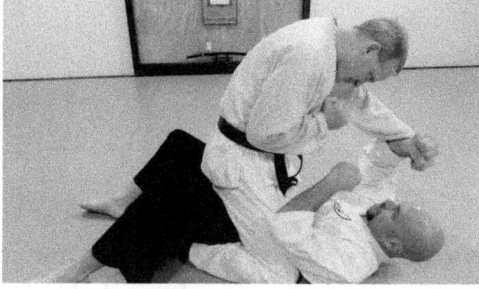

Nage is supine with uke on top in the mount throwing a punch. This is one representation of the triangle on the ground.

CIRCLE

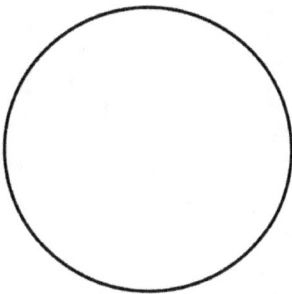

The circle represents completion of technique and the never-ending cycle of movement. Circular movements are found in the application of joint locks, takedowns, evasive movements, and much more. Circles and cycles (spirals) are found throughout nature and form a model for aikido movements.

The circle symbolizes the body-turning movement known as tenkan. In three dimensions, it is a spherical defensive body-turning executed during the process of blending with the energy of the attacker. During newaza, the circle represents the continuous flow of energy between attacker and defender and the wherewithal to use what is given. This is similar to the Japanese concept of In and Yo, (or Yin and Yang in Chinese) in which negative energy directed against a person can be transformed to produce positive opportunites. No matter whether an attacker pushes or pulls in order to apply a technique, yield to the energy, tenkan and evade incoming attacks to off-balance the attacker and apply a counter technique.

The following photos depict the principle of the circle

Uke and nage engage in the clinch

Uke pushes, so nage yields and redirects him | Uke pulls nage, so nage enters and off-balances him

When drawing a circle, a calligrapher begins the stroke and does not stop until the circle is complete. The brush stroke is smooth and continuous. The production of a true circle flows from the unity of mind and body, known as spirit. The same is true for aikido movements.

SQUARE

The square represents the way of stability and control. It signifies a strong connection with the earth, the foundation for all martial techniques including throwing and pinning. Aikidoka who train in newaza realize that the square represents the stability offered by the ground and defenses against any such ground defense positions. The sangen square, as it pertains to newaza, is also about using mass, gravity and one's hara, or center of gravity, to compress, anchor, and immobilize an attacker.

Nage is flat on his back and has uke in the open guard

Uke is flat on his back and nage is in the mount position

In the above photos take notice on how the square is represented. In the first photo nage uses the stability of the floor to hold uke in the guard. In the second photo, nage, who is on top, uses his center and gravity to hold down uke. The Guard will be discussed in the upcoming chapter titled "Ground Defense Positions."

Philosophically, the square reminds us that the body is where the mind and spirit manifest. As we feel a physical attack with our bodies, so too can we display harmful bodily symptoms after a psychological attack. The body is where all aspects of self come together.

Except for blending with the void

There is no way to understand

the Way of Aiki

Poetic Songs of the Way
Morihei Ueshiba (1883-1969)
Aiki News No. 46 March, 15, 1982

Newaza—Not!

Depending on the circumstances, the ground may not be where you want to be during an altercation. As mentioned in **"Strategic Insights of Mukei No Ryu aikido,"** the ideal situation is to defend yourself from a standing position, or if you are taken to the ground, to get up as soon as possible. The following scenarios are examples of when it might be disadvantageous to willingly have a confrontation on the ground.

Suppose you find yourself surrounded by two or more attackers in an isolated area, where it is unlikely that anyone will come to your rescue. One person strikes first. You take this person down and establish a top mount position on the attacker. Obviously, mobility on the ground is limited, and you are exposed to attacks from the other assailants. Newaza has limited effectiveness against multiple attackers; randori training will better serve you as a way of evading attacks and exiting the area. To put it bluntly, run for your life!

One-on-one attacks can occur in places where the environment itself might be dangerous. An assailant might attack in an area that contains broken glass and other sharp debris. Defending yourself from a standing position would prevent unnecessary injury. In this vein, if you take down the assailant, he may likely suffer an injury from the debris in addition to any harm sustained from the fall itself.

What about an attack in shallow water? In this case, by going to the ground with the assailant, you risk being drowned.

Andrade-Shihan taken at the cumpleañero party

More commonly encountered is the infamous barroom brawl. In this actual example, the evening began innocently enough as a birthday party was being celebrated at a crowded Latin nightclub. Friends and relatives sat at one big table. Many were already thoroughly inebriated. At the midnight hour, in what seemed like a good idea, some of the partiers threw water at the head of the birthday celebrant (cumpleañero). The water splashed some of the people at a nearby table. The people at the table complained; apologies were offered and not accepted. Mayhem ensued. The wife of the cumpleañero attacked a wet female bystander, and the two wrestled on the floor. The cumpleañero's brother-in-law knocked the other peoples' table and threw a chair, injuring another bystander's head. Another celebrant threw a bottle, missing some other people. Others joined in to create a general melee with some of the fighters grappling on the floor. Finally, bouncers intervened and restored order. The alcohol-influenced reason for the attack was because of unaccepted apologies.

At the first sign of trouble, Andrade-Shihan removed himself from the quarrel and did not intervene. He watched the chaos unfold from a safe position. Afterward, some wondered why he did not step in and use his aikido. The reasons were sober intelligence and aikido ethics. This situation was not about self-defense. A wise martial artist knows when and how to use what he has learned for the greater good. A tactical observation is in order: in a drunken, chaotic environment in which space is severely limited and the number of attackers multiply with each passing moment, neither tachiwaza nor newaza may be appropriate or effective. Let the bouncers earn their pay.

Newaza for Children

Newaza is an extremely fun activity to channel the seemingly limitless energy of children. When newaza is taught as part of a children's aikido curriculum, the youngsters learn to express themselves in a creative way through movement. The mental and physical challenges stimulate their analytical minds and develop their ability to improvise.

The physical rigors of newaza make it a great way to improve a child's conditioning. It can also be practiced year-round, while other seasonal sports cannot. Aikido classes that include newaza are an excellent alternative to having a child sit around watching TV or playing video games; there is real interaction with other real children. If a child is not inclined to participate in team sports, then newaza may be a positive alternative. Let's face it, most kids love to wrestle around, so why not give them the opportunity to do something that they enjoy in a controlled environment.

Earning ranks and/or belts in aikido can give children confidence and a sense of accomplishment. Although it is not the main objective or focus of training, these acknowledgements of their achievements help them to set attainable goals and motivate them to work toward refining their skills. Aikido newaza is one way in which children can see the positive results of their efforts in action. They realize that with effort comes reward. This is an invaluable lesson for their schooling and for life in general.

Parents often wonder, "Is it advisable for children to participate in organized competitive sports?" Sports such as football, baseball, basketball and soccer train youth in the admirable qualities of discipline and teamwork. Children experience both individual and group accomplishment; they learn to handle both success and failure since there are "winners" and "losers." A sense of sportsmanship helps the young athlete mature by teaching respect for others by realizing that there is always another game, and next time the result may be different. Since, in a game, there is something at stake, that stress can inspire a young player to perform from the deep level of the body-mind and experience the timeless flow of living and executing in the moment. In aikido, this is called takemusu aiki.

But competition is not the be-all and end-all of life. It is not the only way in which we define ourselves. The downside of organized competitive sports is that children may become highly aggressive, less empathetic, more egotistical, and less generous. Parents and coaches are responsible for minimizing these less-than desirable qualities.

One way of ensuring that children find a balance in their lives is to encourage them to participate in cooperative activities. Most aikido schools do not teach their art as a competition. Rather, aikido instructors foster a noncompetitive, more cooperative, environment, to teach a standard martial arts curriculum that may include newaza. Aggression is reduced by allowing no contests, no comparing of oneself to others, and in a more positive vein, teaching the youngster to have compassion for his or her training partners. The child aikidoka learns respect and care for his friends, family, environment and himself. He or she becomes more aware, more safety-conscious, and more comfortable with working in close contact with other students. Once again, aikido and newaza are simply fun activities that can be enjoyed with other participants. For these reasons and many more, aikido newaza provides a cooperative counterbalance to a world that is often centered on competition.

Another consideration that no parent can ignore is the potential problem of bullying. Bullies often prey on insecure and physically smaller children. Training in aikido and newaza can help a bullied child defend against these predators. Not only does aikido teach useful self-defense techniques, but it also gives children the confidence to stand up for themselves. Sometimes this is all a child needs to dissuade a bully from harassing him or her. Bullies do not like resistance. The following anecdote is illustrative.

Nemeroff-Shihan had a student who, for years, was regularly picked on by a bully who was larger and in a higher grade than him. For this reason, the student hated school. In an attempt to stop his torment, his parents enrolled him in Nemeroff-Shihan's dojo over the summer. His goal was to learn how to protect himself before he would meet up with the bully during the upcoming school year.

When September arrived and the school year began, the student walked into the restroom one day only to find his bully waiting for him. The bully pushed him up against the wall but never expected what was about to transpire. Nemeroff's student set the bully off balance, hit him in the stomach, and then executed a shihonage (four winds throw) sending the bully reeling into a restroom stall. The bully never bothered the student again. Although the use of martial skills should always be a last resort and ought not to be encouraged, sometimes using such skills is necessary so as not to live in fear and survive.

Here follows several skill development exercises that can be incorporated into a children's newaza curriculum. In keeping with aikido philosophy, these exercises are taught in a noncompetitive manner, without rewarding the participants. The children should just enjoy the process of the games.

NEWAZA GAMES FOR CHILDREN

Have children form into pairs at one end of the mat. Both partners should be next to each other and on their hands and knees. One student has to try to crawl across the mat and touch the other side. The other partner has to attempt to prevent the first partner from reaching the other side by pinning, grappling and/or holding the student until he cannot go any farther and taps out.

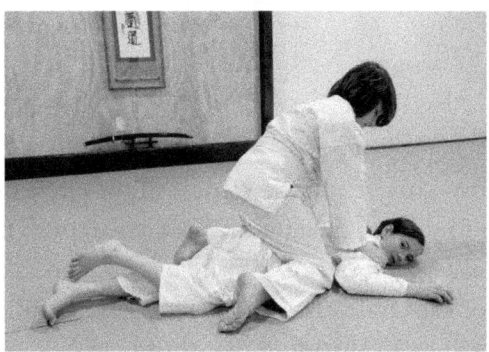

Have the children kneel in a circle. Place two children in the middle of the circle on their knees. Each of the two children in the middle of the circle should try to push or pull the other out of the circle. The first child forced out of the circle returns to take a place in the circle, and another member of the circle takes her place in the middle. Repeat until all children have had a chance to be in the middle of the circle.

The above sample of aikido newaza games can give children confidence in a fun and safe environment. Such games help develop motor skills, physical coordination, and problem-solving skills similar to those utilized in a chess match. As young students enjoy all phases of aikido newaza training, they will often develop greater self-esteem that can positively influence their personal growth.

All in all, aikido newaza training is appropriate, safe, and beneficial to children of various ages and body types. It can improve a child's interpersonal skills and lay a foundation for a better future. Martial arts are not just for adults.

A person who

In any situation

Perceives the truth with resignation

Would never need to draw his sword in haste

> Poetic Songs of the Way
> Morihei Ueshiba (1883-1969)
> Aiki News No. 46 March, 15, 1982

The Importance of Posture and Stances

A person's posture is sometimes the first impression and initial engagement into a fighting situation. A stance can exude confidence or show signs of fear. It is a reflection of your inner emotional frame of mind. A correct posture also provides a solid foundation from which to evade attacks and remain standing.

Aikido stances and footwork enable the defender to evade strikes and to enter into safe strategic positions. Tenkan and irimi facilitate maintaining proper distance and an ability to redirect oncoming attacks. Moving in such a way as to blend with the energy of the attacker while not resisting the attack, allows the defender to retaliate with an effective immobilization, takedown, or other escape options.

According to Mukei No Ryu aikido principles, while a potential adversary remains at a distance beyond striking range, the aikidoka should refrain from raising his or her arms into a defensive posture. Such a stance would signal to the adversary one's martial knowledge and an intention to respond aggressively. This makes de-escalation of a confrontational situation difficult, if not impossible.

Instead, the aikidoka remains relaxed with his or her arms at the side as demonstrated in the photograph below. As the adversary closes the distance to the aikidoka, he or she can enter obliquely to meet the attack or tenkan to redirect it. In either case, one can also use these entries to land into the clinch position. From the clinch, the setup for newaza can begin.

An aikidoka is always connected to the ground for stability and balance. The ground provides a taproot for his or her many movements of ki. A tree draws nutrients from the ground. A house is strongest when its foundation is strong. Even a baby wiggles and crawls on the ground before standing upright. Likewise, a martial artist is most effective when grounded in a strong stance and spiraling ki from the ground upward throughout the body. When upright and moving, the aikidoka slides his or her feet so as to remain connected to the ground.

Aikido techniques are performed while totally relaxed, but not limp. At the same time, structural support and power should be evident in one's erect posture and flowing movements. In fact, all balance and flowing movements originate from a person's hara.

One such popular posture amongst aikidoka is the harmonious or complimentary stance known as ai hanmi. The aikido-ka appears in the left triangular stance. This stance may vary slightly from one aikido school to the next. In a Mukei No Ryu aikido left triangular stance, the left foot should point forward while the right-rear foot points to the right oblique. The pattern is reversed for a right triangular stance. The feet should be fairly close together, about shoulder width apart, with knees slightly bent. A benefit of a triangular stance's narrow footing is that the aikidoka is less rooted in place, allowing for quick evasive movements in many different directions.

An erect posture is essential for good balance and strong ki flow. It is important to keep your chin tucked slightly. Some wrestlers and grapplers tend to lean forward and crouch low to maintain a low center of gravity. Some even start a defense by kneeling on one knee while protruding their head forward with the back bent.

The disadvantage of such a posture is that extending the head forward leaves the wrestler's head exposed to a strike. This may be suited for sporting events in which strikes are not allowed, but it is not safe for a real-life confrontation.

If you have fallen to the ground, it is important to know how to regain your footing and arise to resume the triangular stance. At first, you are on the ground and off-balance. Protect your vital areas against further attack.

Reestablish firm contact with the ground as you continue to protect yourself.

Move into a low, stable stance from which you can either escape the attacker by performing a forward roll or rise up to the triangular stance to face the attacker.

Finally, raise yourself into the triangular stance and ready position.

Causing the perverted enemy to attack

I must then stand behind his form

And so cut the enemy down.

> Poetic Songs of the Way
> Morihei Ueshiba (1883-1969)
> Aiki News No. 46 March, 15, 1982

Mukei No Ryu's Categorization of Newaza

Many techniques and evasive strategies comprise Mukei No Ryu's general curriculum. Within this inventory, newaza has its own niche. Categories of techniques for newaza include shimewaza, kansetsuwaza, osaewaza, and atemiwaza. To fully understand the scope of newaza, one should have a working knowledge of each of these categories.

Shimewaza is the application of choking (circulatory) and strangulation (respiratory) techniques. Such techniques can abruptly and totally stop the flow of blood to the brain and/or deprive the brain of needed oxygen. Loss of consciousness due to the application of a circulatory choke can occur in as little as four seconds. Unconsciousness resulting from a respiratory choke can be rendered within ten seconds. Other effects of applying chokes or strangulations are painful pressure to nerve bundles, hyperflexion, hyperextension, and/or hyper-rotation of the neck with torque and pressure upon the cervical spine.

Before dangerous techniques like chokes and strangulations are taught, the sensei must thoroughly explain how, why, and under what circumstances it is proper to apply such techniques as well as the physical risks and legal ramifications involved. Since loss of consciousness, permanent injury, and even death from a choke can happen in a matter of seconds, the sensei must be extremely observant during the entire process. As stated previously, uke must tap out immediately as the technique is applied. Uke must not allow time for sufficient pressure to mount to the point of causing problems such as light-headedness or dizziness.

We must emphasize that shimewaza is never to be taught to children and/or anyone harboring a violent or aggressive disposition. Furthermore, do not teach shimewaza to novice students until they have proven themselves as responsible, considerate, and able to maintain control while executing techniques. Training with shimewaza as part of an aikido class is not playtime.

Other catagories of techniques include kansetsuwaza that refers to joint manipulation techniques commonly performed on fingers, wrists, elbows, shoulders, ankles, knees and osaewaza includes pinning, holding, and restraining techniques executed to control and immobilize an assailant. What makes these techniques so effective is that their application often creates significant pain by pinching a nerve and/or over stretching the body's connective tissue to the above-mentioned anatomical areas. When any techniques from these categories are applied to a point beyond the natural range of motion of one or more joints (hyperextension, hyperflexion, and/or hyperrotation) severe damage may result. This could be one reason why these techniques are restricted in some MMA competitions.

Atemi, or striking, can be considered an art unto itself, however it is also a part of effective aikido training. When performing atemi, it is essential to have some understanding of human anatomy and physiology. Understanding how the body will react differently when struck in different areas will allow you to develop a more pragmatic strategy. It is also important to understand skeletal anatomy. If a strike is executed without proper structural alignment of the joints, an injury to the wrist or knuckles can occur to the striker instead of the person being struck.

Besides the obvious physical damage, an atemi can off balance and distract the attacker. As a result, it may take some time for the attacker to recover from the pain and confusion caused by the strike. This allows the defender to evade, escape or to counterattack.

The inclusion of strikes while ground grappling is the first step to transitioning from a grappling sport to a practical self-defense curriculum. If taken to the ground or if a grappling situation occurs, it is easy to get caught up in the wrestling mentality. Do not try to fight fire with fire. As the attacker tries to restrain you, strike him in as many vital areas as possible. This will often stun the person and cause him to temporarily loosen his hold on you. This short window of opportunity can allow you to escape, execute your own technique, and possibly return to the safer standing position. Furthermore, atemi may hold the key to survival on the ground with an attacker who is proficient in grappling arts or even someone who is just bigger and stronger. If you do not study and practice the art of atemi diligently to the full potential, you may not be fully prepared to defend yourself in any situation or position including the ground.

Knowledge of certain newaza techniques and in which category it resides is helpful in attaining an overall understanding of Mukei No Ryu aikido newaza. It will also help you become a well-rounded martial artist. Use the still photographic breakdown of our ground techniques in this book and the dynamic video on the companion DVD to learn to match technique to category.

Ground Defense Positions

Since newaza is a like a chess match in which one wrong move can bring about capture of an asset or the restriction of its movement, advantageous positioning is crucial to success. As the attacker moves, nage must sense what he has planned, visualize the bigger picture, and hopefully see a few moves ahead to set up the finish. From a dominant position, nage can tie up the attacker, execute a submission, and even go for a knockout with strikes. Proper positioning can ultimately lead to the proverbial checkmate.

Nage is on the bottom and has uke in the closed guard   Nage is in the top mount position

Effective ground defense requires understanding of the guard, the mount, and the use of their respective variations. It is also important to learn how to execute and escape from each of these positions.

These positions are not unique to our Mukei No Ryu aikido, they are also used in other martial arts such as Judo, MMA, jujutsu, and others. The primary positions of effective ground defense are referred to as the trunk pin, or guard and the vertical four-directional hold, or mount and their variations. In this chapter, we only demonstrate a few examples. It is important to learn how to execute and master the necessary pins to effectively control and immobilize your opponent, and prevent any escapes and/or counters.

Trunk Pin/Guard

In the trunk pin (guard), one person is lying supine. The other person sits, kneels, or stands between the supine person's legs. If the person lying supine wraps the other person's torso with ankles locked, this is a closed guard. If the legs are not wrapped, it is an open guard. A smaller defender, who is taken to the ground, is more likely to end up in the supine position and be held there due to the greater physical strength of the larger attacker. Much practice should be devoted to striking, locking, and choking from this orientation as well as escaping from the pin and transitioning from the ground to a standing position.

It may be easier and safer for nage to defend his position by having uke in the guard while wrapping uke's torso very tightly to restrict mobility. This allows nage continued use of both arms for blocking a strike or applying a submission hold with the idea of reversing and escaping the attack. This position also provides stability by keeping the feet flat and knees bent (open guard). Keeping the feet flat on the floor can provide a foundation from which to push off with sufficient force to unbalance the attacker.

VERTICAL FOUR-DIRECTION HOLD/TOP FULL MOUNT

In this position, uke lies supine while nage sits straddling his torso. This dominant position allows more mobility and added power from gravity to perform downward strikes, and the ability to use one's weight to anchor the attacker to the ground. Using the thighs to squeeze uke's torso further constrains his movement and the ability to breathe freely. From this position, nage can employ submissions and keep uke on the defensive. In the top full mount, nage can be situated low over uke's abdomen or high over uke's chest close to his neck. It is best to mount where the chest and/or the abdominal circumference is less prominent and make sure your knees and dorsal aspect of your feet make contact with the ground. The pressure felt by being forced to take purely defensive actions, can prompt an error from which uke may not recover.

Nage in the top full mount

A variation of the top full mount.

When nage mounts uke, he should keep a low center of gravity. It is harder for uke to execute an escape, and possibly a reversal when nage is in a high position. Keeping this in mind, drop and stabilize the hara when assuming the hold. Harnessing your weight to compress uke's body not only restricts possible movements, but also drains uke of energy while he or she tries to escape. A fatigued attacker is a weaker attacker.

When attempting to apply a grappling technique from this position, keep the head down and close to the side of uke's head for protection to maintain a low center of gravity. The higher, and therefore more exposed nage's head is, the easier it is to hit.

Half Mount

The half mount is a variation of the top mount characterized by placing one knee on the ground or on uke's chest or abdomen while extending the other leg for increased stability.

CROSS MOUNT/SIDE FOUR CORNER HOLD

To secure a cross mount, nage lies chest down on top of, and perpendicular to uke's chest. Nage's legs should be spread wide to give added stability. Uke's distant arm should be hugged near the shoulder for better control. The cross mount has proven to be a good transitional hold as nage moves from one position to another. However, possibilities for submissions from this position should not be overlooked.

During the cross mount, nage sinks his weight on uke's chest to limit mobility and to bring about fatigue. Nage should not overextend his or her body across uke's body, or the opponent could escape and reverse positions.

When a technique like ikkyo or sankyo is applied correctly, it is likely that he may end up prone on the mat and tapping as the technique is applied. However, with a takedown like this, new students often instinctually fall to their back, so they can see what is coming next and possibly counter it. Unfortunately, many aikido schools intentionally teach their students to be compliant throughout the technique and remain in the prone position, cooperative without resisting, until their partner completes a final immobilization. By doing this he becomes a sacrificial lamb. Remaining prone and compliant creates an opening for someone to apply the rear full mount, which is one of the worst positions to be in. This kind of practice is not honest, genuine and certainly not practical or an advanced form of training. It definitely does not train the student's mind for self-defense in the streets. It does shugyo and takemusu aiki a disservice.

REAR FULL MOUNT

The rear full mount is considered to be the most advantageous and dominant ground defense position. It is characterized by having one person behind the other. When both persons are in the prone position, the person on top is in an advantageous position. When both persons are in the supine position, the person on the bottom is the advantageous position.

In aikido, ushirowaza, or techniques performed from the rear, are generally not practiced during newaza. They are mostly used as a separate category of empty-handed techniques for the purposes of developing strong zanshin and fomenting a sixth sense. Performing these techniques trains the body-mind to anticipate attacks from all directions, including attacks from behind, to establish harmony and to excel in performing serial technique combinations, counters, and reversals.

In the rear full mount, if the person on the bottom is strong enough to use his legs to get up, retaliate, or escape, the person on top must be ready to simultaneously use his legs to hook the opponent's legs, strike his neck or head, and perform other defenses like a rear triangular choke using his legs and/or a rear naked choke.

Given this scenario, a good alternative would be to perform sankyo to his left hand, since the right leg has already trapped his entire right upper extremity. This position makes it easier for the person on top to get up and defend himself in case multiple attackers come to the rescue of the person on the bottom.

Scarf Hold

In the scarf hold, one person (uke) lies on the ground in the supine position. The person on top (nage) rests on his hip over uke, leaning tightly against him. Nage maintains control by wrapping one arm around uke's neck so as to keep his head off the ground and wraps uke's free arm tightly around his waist. Nage leans forward and grabs high on uke's arm. Nage rotates his body so that uke's right arm is pulled up and his body compresses against uke's chest making it difficult for uke to breathe. Nage can follow up with a strangulation that causes pain to the back of uke's neck. This is accomplished by nage grasping his own hands and pulling upward while applying downward pressure with the rest of his body.

By means of the Way

Call out the misguided enemy

Advance and pursuade him with words of instruction

Through the Sword of Love.

> Poetic Songs of the Way
> Morihei Ueshiba (1883-1969)
> Aiki News No. 46 March, 15, 1982

Newaza Mechanics and the Combination Lock

From the moment, someone enters within striking distance of another person, there is the risk of physical contact, injury, and whether the person is a friend or foe, there is the certainty of an energy exchange. Once there is an interaction with or perception of someone's energy, it triggers numerous unconscious actions from danger assessment, the decision whether or not to allow physical contact, and certain preparatory movements that situate oneself favorably in preparation for physical contact. If the assessment of danger is zero, then a pleasant, friendly, and sought-for contact is about to ensue. A high-danger assessment indicates a darker, likely violent encounter is imminent. Whatever happens next is unknowable. When a violent confrontation cannot be avoided, then all precautions must be taken and all self-defense skills must be on the table for use.

When a fight goes to the ground, the previously mentioned advantageous positions such as the guard or the mount are frequently used in aiki-newaza. From any of these positions, other finishing techniques can be applied to resolve the confrontation favorably. In order to apply any of these techniques successfully, a concept known as the combination lock must be utilized. Brief mentions of these steps have been made previously. Here we will examine the steps of the combination lock more thoroughly.

The steps of the combination lock are named redirection, compression, constriction, and application. Knowledge of these steps helps martial arts students break down newaza and understand what makes the techniques work in real life. Each step of the combination lock brings nage greater control and closer to finishing the techniques. Once these steps are mastered, they become a natural part of each technique and should flow from one movement to the next. Understand that although we separate these steps for the purpose of explanation, the principles and application of the combination lock to any technique should happen in a matter of seconds. Here follow the steps of the combination lock.

Redirection

When uke initiates an attack and nage intercepts it, redirection commences. This is also the point at which altering the attacker's balance (kuzushi) comes into play. Nage meets the strike (punch or kick) while it is in motion in order to merge his energy with the energy of the strike and redirect it. During this energetic encounter, nage moves out of the power zone of the strike so as not to block the strike directly with full force. This action ensures that nage does not absorb the full energy of the attack.

The above series of photos demonstrate Redirection in action. Uke delivers a straight punch, nage redirects uke in a spiral movement to dissipate the force of the attack downward

In a scenario where uke and nage enter a clinch, pushing and/or pulling is likely to happen, even after both are on the ground. In aikido, the redirection continues as nage resists the temptation to fight the forces of pushing and/or pulling. Instead, nage allows

these forces to dissipate as he or she leads uke into a disadvantageous position.

The following series of photos demonstrates the principle of the Redirection from the mount position. Uke, who is on the bottom, attempts to strike nage. As the strike is executed, nage parrys and redirects the force of the attack to his right. Nage continues to extend uke's attack in order to roll him onto his stomach and apply an ikkyo.

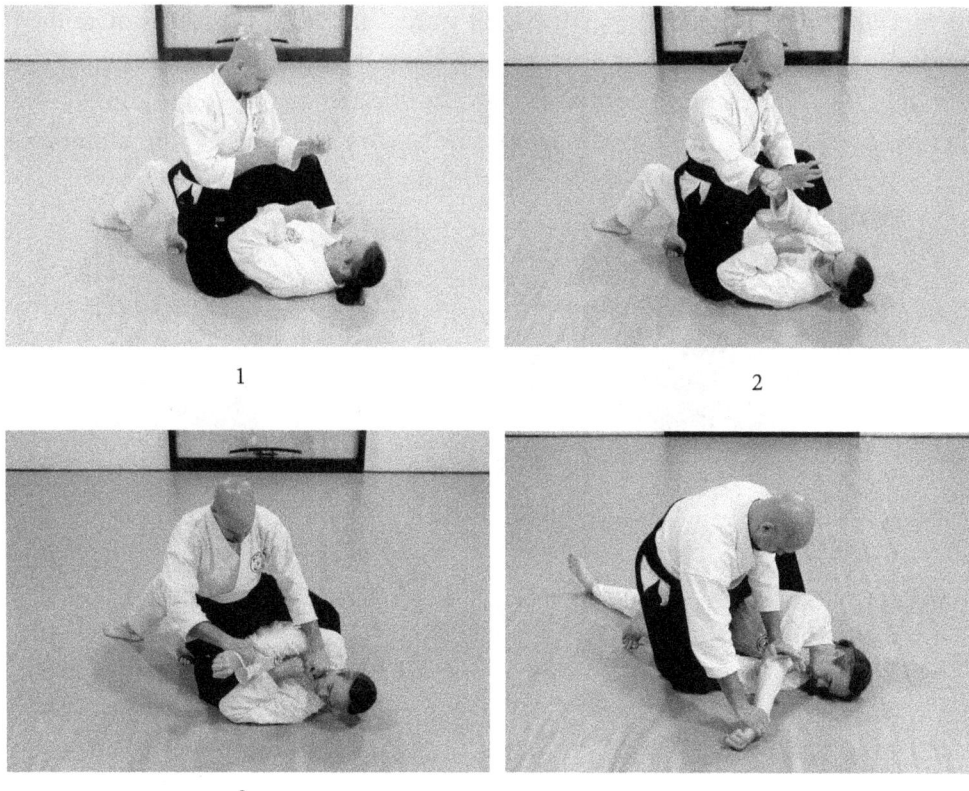

COMPRESSION

After redirecting uke's attack, the next step in executing the combination lock is compression. When nage and uke are on the ground and nage is in the guard, the mount or any hold where nage is on top, downward compression anchors uke to limit mobility and restricts his or her ability to escape from these positions. Nage should settle his weight and use gravity to his advantage. To accomplish this settling, nage must relax his or her body. Imagine lying on the ground supine with a large bag of water on top of you. Nage is that bag of water. This effect becomes magnified if nage, with feet secured to the ground, pushes his or her body downward against uke. This affords nage a few more seconds to stabilize uke and complete a technique. Even when nage must move and/or change position, compression is to be maintained. Compression can physically and mentally fatigue an opponent.

1. Notice nage on top with his hips too high. This allows uke to escape.

2. Nage drops his hips downward and applies the Compression correctly.

CONSTRICTION

The purpose of constriction is to restrict uke's ability to take in air and to assist with compression. Constriction causes fatigue, thereby taking the fight out of the attacker and making it easier to apply a technique. Think of how a boa constrictor entwines itself around its prey in order to crush it. As uke exhales and/or shifts position slightly, nage applies greater downward pressure with his or her hips. Nage squeezes uke with his or her extremities, closing any available gaps. As the attacker tries to escape, nage should close remaining openings, tightening his technique. Such constricting will cause uke an increasing difficulty with inhalation resulting in further fatigue and diminished power to fight back. Additionally, it also helps restrict uke's ability to use his extremities.

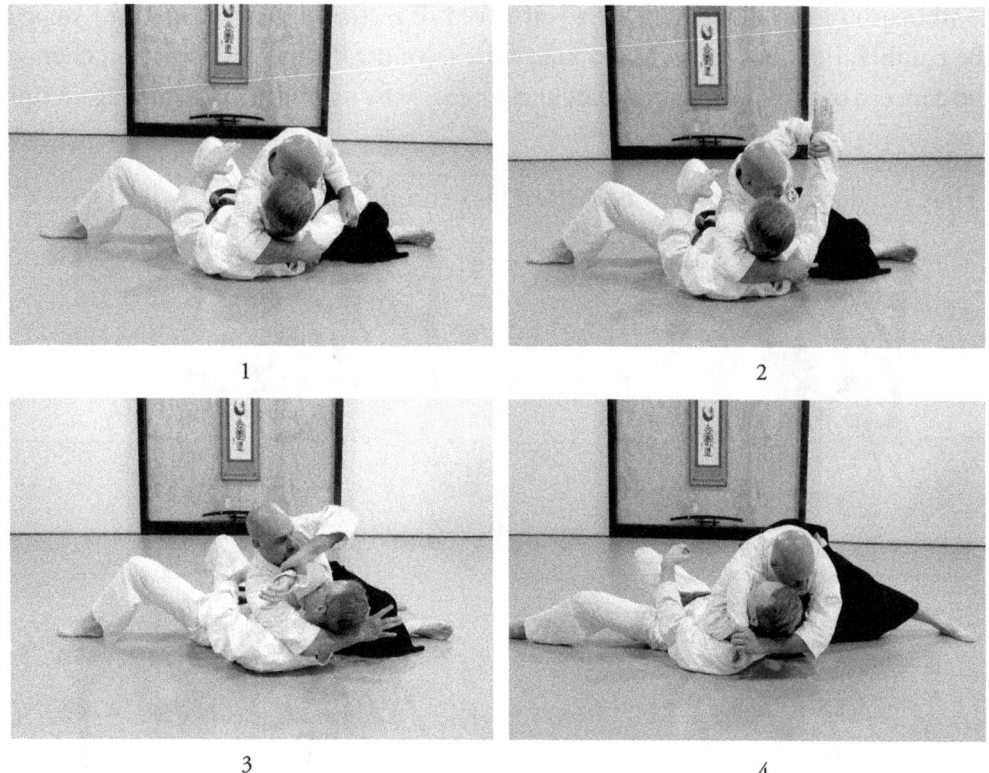

This is a transition from kesa gatame to kata gatame. It is both a pin and a strangulation. Notice how nage continues to wrap up uke with his own arm. During the technique, the arm wrap around the face and neck continues to constrict tighter on both sides of the neck until uke submits.

APPLICATION

Once redirection, compression, and constriction have been executed, nage is ready to apply a finishing technique. Some of the possible finishing techniques will be presented shortly. Application of technique must be done quickly with precision and full commitment and without hesitation. Do not forget to maintain compression and constriction during technique application. No matter which style of newaza you study or which technique you want to use, keep in mind and practice the combination lock. Remember, in a real world of tactical situation, the four steps in the combination lock happen in a matter of seconds. If a ground situation changes, the concept of the Combination Lock will need to be reapplied again and again until a technique is executed successfully.

Here is a depiction of the combination lock through all four steps.

1a 1b

1c 1d

The sequence of the above four photos demonstrate the principle of Redirection

2. Nage applies Compression with his upper torso

3. Nage applies Constriction wrapping aroung uke's arm while maintaining compression

4. Application of this technique is completed with an ikkyo

Suwariwaza and Hanmi Handachiwaza

Traditionally, aikido includes four practices based on being in a ground position; seiza, shikko, suwariwaza and hanmi handachiwaza. The origins of these techniques have an interesting martial history. Today, they are taught more as traditional exercises that help the student balance, center and increase hip strength.

During the Muromachi period (1336-1573 CE), the warlords (shogun) lived in castles within their province where they employed many samurai in their service. Some of these samurai were employed as personal bodyguards to the shogun. All swore fealty to their employer in accordance with the rules of Bushido.

According to ancient rules of conduct, the samurai gathered on the floor of a lower level room where they sat in seiza on thick straw mats while the war lord attended from an upper level room. Seiza, the position in which one kneels on the floor, folds the legs underneath the thighs, rests the buttocks on the heels, and maintains an erect posture, has been one of the traditional formal ways of sitting in Japan.

In order to ambulate from sitting in seiza the samurai had to shikko, or walk while in seiza using their feet and knees. To perform this movement correctly, the heels have to be kept close together as the body moves from the hips as a whole unit. The samurai were able to move forward, backward, side-to-side and circularly.

Requiring the samurai to sit in seiza and only move by knee walking was an astute strategy of the warlord to prevent them from standing and moving rapidly to close the distance. Any intelligent warlord knew that the people with the weapons held the real power in a military and political situation. Thus, a warlord needed a well-compensated and absolutely loyal contingent of bodyguards for his protection.

The seiza position restricts one's movement and sitting for long periods of time can cause loss of blood circulation to the extremities, paresthesia, myalgia, arthralgia, general discomfort in the lower extremities and fatigue. This would have applied to novice warriors, the elderly and especially to samurai who may have been injured from martial practice or actual combat.

Sitting in seiza also deprived the samurai of fast, normal, practical and effective action. The samurai's loyalty and obedience meant that they would fight while knee walking and use suwariwaza if necessary. If and when someone broke their Bushido oath and rose from seiza to fight is unknown.

As an added precaution against rebellion, the warlord demanded of the samurai that he leave his katana (Japanese sword) outside the castle while still allowing him to enter with his wakizashi (short sword). This short sword was no match for the katana wielded by the warlord's bodyguards who protected the shogun from potential assassination by the samurai. In the western United States of America, a similar requirement of turning in their guns to the sheriff was given to all cowboys who entered Dodge City. In the Edo period, all samurai had their katana confiscated by the government for its protection.

In accordance with Japanese samurai tradition and without the implied subservience, an aikidoka may start from seiza, move by shikko, and execute a martial technique from suwariwaza or hanmi handachiwaza. Granted, from a martial standpoint, suwariwaza is probably not very practical. After all, how likely is an attack from someone who is kneeling? Seiza, shikko, and suwariwaza training do improve an aikidoka's hip power, posture, and stability. Learning a technique from a variety of positions helps the student to comprehend how the components of the technique make it work. In addition, if the attacker and defender fall to the ground simultaneously, then proficiency with being in seiza, shikko, and suwariwaza can enable the defender to achieve control of the situation.

Since Mukei No Ryu aikido includes traditional training, practices such as seiza, shikko, suwariwaza, and hanmi handachiwaza have a place in the curriculum. Teaching these techniques to students helps them become comfortable with working from the ground. Suwariwaza and hanmi handachiwaza provide a training transition to newaza. The following techniques demonstrate the application of newaza from suwariwaza and hanmi handachiwaza.

SUWARIWAZA

Technique 1

1. Nage and uke face each other in a sitting position.

2. Uke delivers a yokomenuchi strike, and nage enters omote redirecting the atemi.

3. Nage turns, delivering a left-hand slap to uke's face to unbalance him. Uke falls on his back.

4. Nage moves into a side mount applying compression in order to immobilize uke. Nage begins to apply a bent armlock.

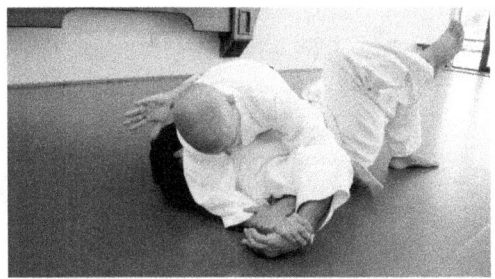

5. Nage moves into a high cross mount, hooks over uke's right shoulder and then under the right arm, to complete a bent armlock.

Technique 2

1. Nage and uke face each other in a sitting position.

2. Nage enters omote and deflects an attempted shoulder grab.

3. Nage grabs uke's left wrist and delivers a left-handed slap to his face. Uke loses balance and falls on his back.

4. Nage begins to control uke by securing his right arm in the half mount position.

5. Nage assumes a top mount and finishes with a bent armlock.

Hanmi Handachiwaza

Technique 1

1. Nage is in a sitting position. Uke, in a standing position, attacks from behind.

2. Uke attempts a rear naked choke, and nage applies sankyo to the middle finger of his right hand.

3. Nage grabs the back of uke's neck with his right hand. Uke loses balance, enabling nage to throw him.

4. Uke performs a breakfall. Nage maintains the sankyo, forcing uke to roll onto his left side.

5. Nage applies a gokyo from a north-south position.
Uke's right arm wraps across his face and nage applies downward pressure to his right, bent wrist.

Technique 2

1. Nage in seiza, faces uke standing

2. Nage deflects uke's attempted grab, delivers a left front kick to his abdomen and strikes his left temple simultaniously.

3. Nage enters, grabs, and pulls uke's right ankle. Uke loses balance and falls onto his back.

4. Nage stands up and uses his right forearm to reach under uke's right ankle and grabs the top of his left wrist.

5. Nage arches his back to apply more pressure and to gain greater leverage as he cradles his right arm under uke's Achilles tendon, trapping uke's right ankle on the back side of nage's armpit to secure the right leg.

Traditional Aikido Newaza

The following ten scenarios of defense demonstrate a sample of the many possible effective applications of traditional aikido techniques utilized within Mukei No Ryu aikido aiki newaza. Each scenario is titled by the featured Aikido technique. In addition to the featured technique, other attacks, immobilizations, pins, chokes and escapes are used to create dynamic and flowing confrontations with decisive resolutions. Notice how aiki newaza is an extension of the techniques and principles of aikido.

Each scenario is illustrated by sequential photographs of selected movements and techniques that are accompanied by descriptive captions. To see the complete scenarios unfold in continuous action, refer to the companion DVD where each one may be viewed at normal speed and in slow motion for instructional purposes.

Ikkyo

1. Nage stands in a ready posture with left foot forward while facing uke.

2. Uke attacks with a right roundhouse punch to the head. Nage enters diagonally to the inside, intercepts the punch and strikes uke's face.

3. Nage reaches over the top of uke's wrist with his right hand and grabs the wrist.

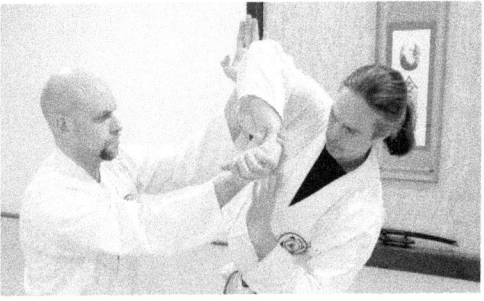

4. Nage raises uke's wrist above his head. Nage places his left hand on uke's elbow and pushes it toward uke's face.

5. Nage steps forward with the left foot while applying downward pressure on uke's elbow, creating an armbar. An effective armbar requires that uke's wrist be held higher than his shoulder.

6. Nage sits down by kicking his left foot forward and applying downward pressure on uke's ribs. Nage also cradles uke's arm to maintain control. Just before nage ends the technique with the ikkyo pin, he changes into waki gatame, or armpit lock. This technique is characterized by trapping uke's arm, applying pressure on the shoulder, and simultaneously locking the shoulder and elbow.

7. Nage elbows uke in the head, causing uke to lift his head and expose his neck. Next, nage wraps his left arm underneath and around uke's neck to grab his right hand. Finally, nage chokes upward against uke's windpipe.

NIKYO

1. Nage and uke face each other in an ai hanmi stance.

2. Uke lunges in at nage and enters the clinch

3. Uke grabs nage and pulls him forward onto the ground.

4. As nage falls into uke's guard, he strikes uke in the throat with his right hand.

5. Uke attempts to strike nage in the face with a right hook punch. Nage deflects the strike with his left hand and reaches over and grabs uke's striking hand and rotates it medially inward so that uke's pinky finger faces upward.

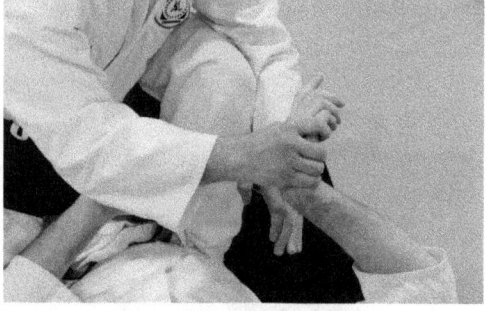

6. Here is a close-up view of the previously described hand position.

7. Nage is in the open guard. He applies a painful nikyo pin by pulling uke's elbow inward while rotating uke's wrist toward his face.

8. Nage pushes uke's elbow forward toward his face, causing him to roll onto his stomach. This leads to an armbar (nikyo) pin.

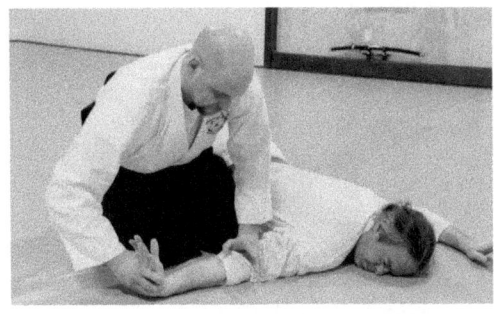 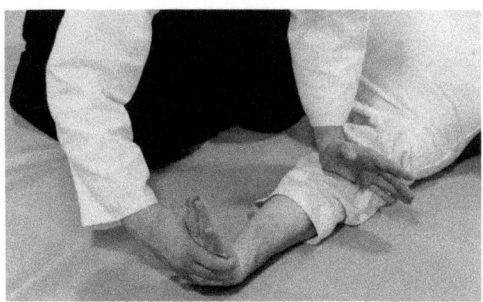

9. Nage pins uke's elbow to the floor by applying downward pressure onto his elbow with a knife hand while at the same time applying inward compression with his hand. This causes pain on uke's elbow and wrist.

10. Here is a close-up view of the previously described wrist pin.

11. Nage prepares to stand up and exit by resting his knee firmly onto uke's elbow while also applying force to uke's face, causing additional pain.

SANKYO

1. Nage and uke face each other in an ai hanmi stance.

2. Uke charges at nage and grabs him.

3. Uke takes nage backward and falls into nage's guard.

4. Uke attempts to strike nage in the face with a straight punch.

5. As uke strikes, nage deflects his punch to the right with his left hand and grabs uke's wrist with his right hand.

6. Nage rotates uke's wrist in a spiral fashion, medially and upward, exposing uke's palm.

7. In order to apply a sanyo pin, nage grabs uke's hand and rotates it to the left, causing pain to the wrist.

8. Nage continues to rotate uke's wrist, forcing uke to roll onto his side in order to avoid further pain.

9. Nage harmonizes with uke's momentum by rolling on top of him and striking him in the face. Nage also continues to hold the sankyo pin with his left hand.

10. As nage sits up, he places his right shin across uke's neck for a choke. At the same time, nage rotates uke's wrist to the left to apply sankyo-induced wrist pain.

11. Before standing up, nage strikes uke in the face with his right hand to stun him.

Yonkyo

1. Nage and uke face each other in an ai hanmi stance.

2. Uke reaches in with his right hand and grabs nage's wrist.

3. As uke moves inward, nage enters to the rear and strikes uke in the ribs.

4. As uke tries to move behind nage to secure an advantageous position and choke him, nage turns to face him.

5. As uke closes in to apply the grab, nage steps in, lowers his center and raises uke's hand upward. This creates the space that allows nage to step underneath his arm.

6. Nage steps underneath uke's arm to move into a safer position. Nage grabs uke's forearm along his radial and ulnar nerves.

7. Nage applies a forward-wringing type motion to uke's forearm, causing pain to uke's arm. This is known as the yonkyo pin.

8. By continuing the pressure downward, uke falls to the floor.

9. Here is a close-up view of the previously described yonkyo pin.

10. From the floor, uke tries to pull nage down on the ground to grapple with him.

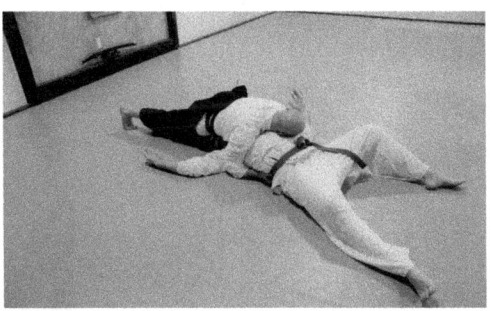

11. In response, nage falls on top of uke in a north-south position, also known as kami shiho gatame.

KAITENNAGE

1. Nage and uke face each other.

2. Uke charges in to take down nage by grabbing his legs. Nage responds by moving to the right oblique angle while deflecting uke's left arm and striking him on the back of his head.

3. Nage grabs uke's left arm and raises it up towards uke's head while bringing uke's head downward in preparation for kaiten nage (rotary throw).

4. Nage executes kaiten nage by continuing the circular rotation of levering uke's arm and pushing down on uke's head.

5. Here is another view of the previously described kaiten nage.

6. Once uke lands, nage controls uke's hand with his left hand.

7. Nage kneels down his inside knee. He moves uke's hand backward towards the top of his head, then grabs his own forearm with his right hand.

8. Nage moves his left foot forward, spreading his legs, so that he can apply downward force to stabilize uke's body. At the same time, nage pushes uke's left hand laterally away from his body, causing pain on the elbow and wrist.

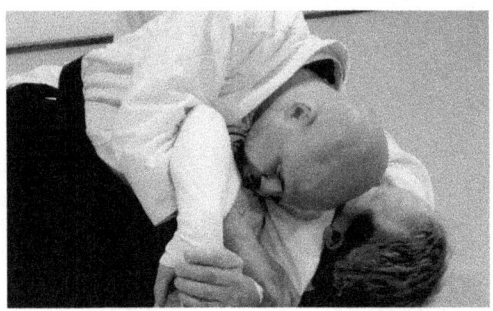

9. Here is a close-up view of the previously described finishing pin.

Kotegaeshi

1. Nage faces uke in preparation for the attack.

2. Uke attacks with a right straight punch to nage's face. Nage evades to the left while deflecting uke's strike with his left hand.

3. Nage attempts to retaliate by striking uke's face. However, uke evades and blocks nage's strike with his left hand.

4. Uke then grabs nage's right hand and rotates it to uke's left to execute a kotegaeshi (wrist twist throw).

5. Uke executes kotegaeshi.

6. Nage falls safely and looks up in expectation of an additional attack.

7. Uke attempts to punch nage in the face with his right hand. Nage shifts to the left, while deflecting uke's punch with his left hand.

8. Nage rotates uke's striking hand to apply pressure to his wrist. At the same time, nage strikes uke in the groin with his right hand, stunning him.

9. Nage starts to apply a one-handed kotegaeshi pin, feeding it towards his leg.

10. Nage wraps his leg around uke's hand, trapping uke's wrist in his knee. It is important for uke's arm to be bent and his wrist to be rotated, so that there is pain.

11. Nage pulls his leg down, causing pain for uke. This makes uke go over.

12. Once uke lands, nage kicks uke in the face with his heel.

13. Nage rolls onto his knee and strikes uke's face with his right hand. Nage maintains control of uke's right arm with his left hand.

Sayuundo

1. Nage faces uke in preparation for an attack.

2. Uke attacks with a roundhouse punch. Nage deflects the punch, enters forward forty five degrees to his right, and strikes uke on the side of his head.

3. Nage parries uke's right hand downward with his left hand and passes it to his right hand.

4. Nage extends his left arm across uke's neck and leans him backward.

5. Nage begins to rotate his hips towards uke while placing his knee behind uke's legs to execute a sayu undo (sideways motion exercise).

6. Nage continues to execute the throw.

7. Nage throws uke over his knee.

8. Once uke lands, nage grabs uke's arm and kicks his face.

9. Nage slides his right leg behind uke's head while pulling up on uke's arm.

10. Nage sits backward and applies downward force on uke's arm against nage's hip, applying hyperextension pain to uke's elbow (juji gatame).

11. Uke tries to sit up and escape, so nage keeps it sticky and applies downward pressure against the back of uke's neck with his right foot.

12. Nage pushes uke's head downward so that he is lying in the prone position. Nage kicks his left leg toward uke's head to sit up.

13. Nage sits up with uke's right arm extended between his legs to execute an armbar.

Kokyunage

1. Nage faces uke in preparation for yokomen uchi attack.

2. Uke attacks with a right round house punch. Nage enters to the right forward oblique angle, while deflecting the punch with his left hand. Nage reaches up to grab the back of uke's head.

3. Nage steps back with his left foot, drawing uke's head and right arm downward.

4. Uke is thrown by continuing the force of his own strike.

5. Uke lands on his side.

6. Once uke lands, he pulls nage down. Nage lands across him and elbows him in the ribs.

7. Then, nage reaches around uke's ankle and pulls it in into external rotation. This causes pain to uke's knee.

Koshinage

1. Nage faces uke in preparation for the attack.

2. Uke lunges in and grabs nage's lapel.

3. Uke spins backward with his left foot and grabs nage's right arm to execute a koshinage (hip throw).

4. Uke successfully executes koshinage.

5. Nage lands from the throw.

6. Uke goes to the ground to attempt a side mount. Nage grabs uke's left arm and elbows uke in the face as he is coming down.

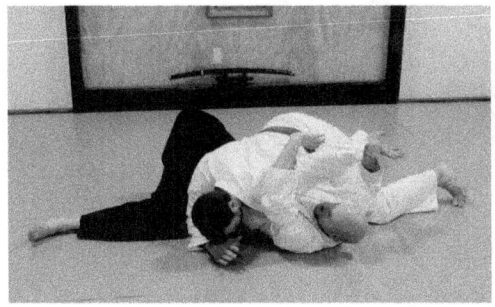

7. Nage grabs uke's left wrist with his right hand while wrapping his left arm around uke's tricep.

8. This is another view of the previously described arm wrap.

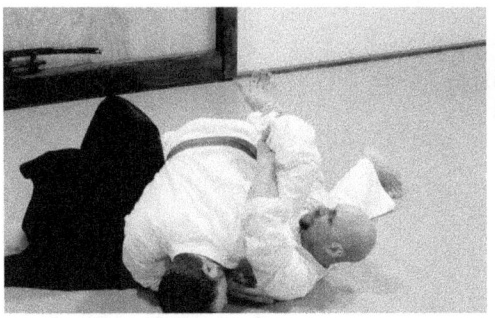

9. Now nage grabs uke's left wrist with his left hand. Nage applies tension to uke's elbow and shoulder by pulling his wrist toward uke's head.

10. Nage rolls to the left, applying pressure to uke's shoulder.

11. By continuing the roll, nage ends up in a cross mount and pulls uke's arm back towards his head, applying a shoulder lock.

12. Here is a close-up view of the previously described shoulder lock.

13. Once uke's shoulder is locked, nage hooks uke's ankle and pulls it into external rotation towards uke's head, causing strain to uke's knee.

Tenchinage

1. Uke grabs nage from behind in a rear bearhug.

2. Nage stomps on uke's foot to loosen the grip.

3. Nage moves his arms forward to break the hold.

4. Nage swipes uke's left arm out of the way as he steps to the left, getting to the outside of uke's hold.

5. Uke grabs nage's wrists in an attempt to control nage.

6. Nage steps forward, separates his arms and executes a tenchinage (heaven and earth throw).

7. Uke is thrown backward.

8. Nage clears uke's left arm with his left arm.

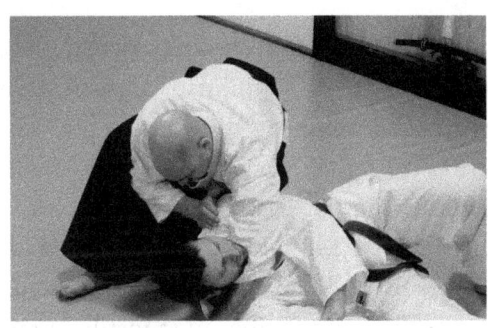

9. Nage kneels down on his left knee and wraps his left arm around uke's neck.

10. Nage sits down and clasps his own hands around uke's neck to complete the choke.

Takin' It to the Street

As students venture beyond the walls of the dojo and into the real world, they must take the lessons he or she has learned and implement them when the proverbial gloves are off and there is no referee. They need to translate them into a physical language that bridges the gap between formal regimented practices of the dojo and the danger that can occur in the concrete jungle. This is a major separation between a martial art and a martial sport and ultimately the underlying message of this book.

Simply put, a martial art is any of several arts of combat that encompass a self-defense strategy. Once an art is taught with no grounding in combat, it is no longer a martial art. Except for military combat training, very few hand-to-hand and weapons-styles are taught as true martial arts. For example, modern competitive wushu (kung fu) is often performed as a martial, gymnastic sport. Shin Shin Toitsu (Ki Society), derived from Ueshiba's aikido, incorporates kiatsu, or life-energy therapy. Tai Chi is mostly taught as a fitness and well-being program. There is nothing wrong with this approach. This evolution of the martial way has successfully brought varying levels of martial skill to the general public through self-defense training, sport/entertainment and health practices.

Aikido was originally created as a martial way. Many aikido techniques were derived from various Japanese fighting arts including Daito-ryu aikijujutsu, a particularly brutal martial art. Although O'Sensei eliminated some of the most lethal and damaging techniques of Daito-ryu, he retained a collection of effective techniques that complemented his spiritual vision. Like the other martial arts, aikido evolved into a combination of self-defense training, enlightenment art, and fitness program. Aikido is usually taught in such a way that it is impossible to separate these components from each other. However, effective aikido self-defense training must instill certain fundamental martial methods and dispense with some forms of dojo etiquette that contradict the cultivation of effective self-preservation. The following ideas will shed a light on the self-defense mind-set of practical aikido.

In order to successfully prepare for the streets, students must first be able to control their fear. It is almost impossible to totally eliminate it, but there are essential practices that can be utilized to minimize it. Keep in mind that if fear gains a hold, then hesitation, flinching, cowering, and/or submissive behaviors emerge and in so doing, defeat is likely. Since most students know, even if only subconsciously, that their fellow classmates are not really trying to hurt and or kill them in the dojo setting, some might say that there can never really be true preparation for a violent attacker. Regardless of how prepared you may be, no one can predict any outcome. It all depends on the overall circumstances and the preparation of the individual. It is the theater of the unexpected.

Regular conditioning in meditative and breath control methods practiced while partners attempt to strike each other can help relax the body and mind to achieve a calm-centered mental state that can help suppress fear until the job is done. Having students perform ki-ai while they attack and being conditioned to accept strikes after years of training are other avenues that assist with preventing fear from taking over.

Besides controlling one's anxiety, in order to successfully defend oneself from an attack, your training must have some level of realism. Punching and kicking air does not prepare you to handle a violent situation. Punching bags and dummies do not punch back. Only practice with another person can provide a sufficiently realistic simulation of a tactical situation. Several striking arts employ sparring sessions in which two competitors try to land punches and kicks to amass points. The grappling arts pit two people against each other, each trying to pin and/or submit the other fighter. Aikido training has more in common with grappling training. The level of realism can run the gamut from no resistance to significant resistance, especially during newaza practice.

Realistic aikido training should incorporate more than static wrist grab techniques and defenses against only one type of attack. Aikidoka should practice against a variety of uncontrived attacks including jabs, kicks, grapples, weapons, and so on. Some level of resistance must be included. Aikido practiced without spirit, intensity, and heart is nothing more than physical exercise. A person must become comfortable in the uncomfortable.

Initially, novice students cannot be expected to defend themselves against hard, fast attacks. The neophyte must be brought along slowly and safely. Attacks should begin slowly and increase in speed only as the student gains proficiency and confidence in his or her ability to defend against the attacks. As the partner supplies more energy to attacking, the defender will find it easier and more effective to move in harmony with the partner's energy and redirect the attack.

If aikido training is to be effective, then some common practices must be questioned. As stated earlier, if etiquette interferes with safety, it must be abandoned. For example, there was an aikidoka having several years of training in Orlando, Florida who was attacked by a mugger while using an ATM. The knife-wielding mugger was successfully thwarted. However, due to the aikidoka's training, he unwittingly returned the knife to the mugger. He was attacked a second time and fortunately again prevailed and disarmed the mugger. The aikidoka did not repeat his inappropriate display of dojo etiquette. Such misplaced manners could have cost him his life. In fact, there is another story of a female Asian aikidoka who did the same thing, but she was not as lucky and was killed. The way to eliminate this inappropriate mind-set is to treat every attack by your training partner as though it is an attack by a mugger. While we should honor tradition, we should not do so to the extent that it ignores the dangers of the real world.

Once, Nemeroff-Shihan received a phone call from a potential student inquiring about his dojo. The caller relayed that she had trained in the martial arts for over a year, and her dojo was closing, so she was searching for a new school. She wanted to know the difference between the karate she studied and aikido. When Nemeroff-Shihan described aikido and what was involved in training, she said, "Oh no, I don't want to learn self-defense, I just want karate like my old dojo. We only practiced kata by ourselves." He replied that this was not the dojo for her, but she was welcome to visit if her goals changed.

There are skeptics who say aikido looks more like a dance and that the attacker allows the defender to throw him. The reason for this skepticism is that some schools of aikido do not train in practical aikido. Some styles focus mostly on the spiritual and "art" aspects while dismissing the importance of martial applications. As will become apparent, Mukei No Ryu aikido is not about being a dance school where techniques are practiced without power. If someone wants to dance in other schools, it is of no concern to the authors. Nevertheless, when aikido is done correctly with energy, it might still look like a dance. So be it!

A final word on the subject of dancing and martial arts fighters: In the most anticipated sporting spectacle of recent times, undefeated quintuple champion Floyd Mayweather Jr. defeated UFC MMA fighter Conor McGregor making his boxing debut, via technical knockout in the 10th round. In sealing his 50th straight victory, Mayweather paid tribute to the MMA fighter, "Tonight, I chose the right dance partner!"

There are many martial arts, self-defense styles and even enlightenment styles that can be effective in a tactical situation. No one style or system is the best under all types of attacks. Any person who has been victorious in battle may eventually lose. O'Sensei knew he was no match against the skills of his teacher Sokaku Takeda. Helio Gracie, founder of Gracie Jiu-Jitsu, lost to one of his students, Valdamar Santana, in Brazil after a three hour, forty-five-minute nonstop match. (Martial Arts Legends Magazine, "Martial Arts Legends Magazine presents Gracie Jiu Jitsu," February 1997, p. 21.) Even the legendary ronin Minamoto Musashi, was defeated by Muso Gonnosuke in a second bujutsu duel.

The point is there is always someone with more skill. Yet, even the most skillful person can lose to a less skilled one. Having a lack of stamina, a momentary lack of awareness or feeling ill are good reasons why one might not succeed. All you can do is train each time to the best of your ability with a beginner's mind.

If you consider aikido to be an authentic self-defense martial art suitable for survival purposes, then newaza cannot be overlooked as part of your training. When a fight goes to the ground it remains dynamic. If the attacker escapes a pin, then the aikidoka must respond with newaza skills in the flow of the action. Such a spontaneous, creative use of techniques to help you regain control is the hallmark of takemusu aiki. When defending oneself while in the state of takemusu aiki, self-defense is done without malice or the need to do more harm than necessary. Still, if it is necessary to break an attacker's wrist that is better than taking his life. Your body-mind will make that decision in light of the ethics of your aikido training and the situation.

The following simulated real-world scenarios of attack and defense demonstrate the spontaneity and martial effectiveness of the next stage of ground grappling, which is advanced Mukei No Ryu aikido aiki newaza. The scenarios highlight certain kinds of attacks in various locations and illustrate even more of the numerous aiki newaza responses that are available to a well-trained aikidoka. While the fighting sequences were initially staged by Andrade-Shihan, many of his movements and techniques arose spontaneously as the situations unfolded. To add a sense of realism and inspiration, uke was asked to add resistance to each encounter.

In the following aiki newaza scenarios, you will observe many technical elements of classical aikido as well as techniques with roots in aiki-jujutsu. This presentation includes many different ground defense positions such as the guard, top mount, half mount, rear mount, cross mount and scarf hold etc. In addition, you will observe the clinch and many escapes and submissions such as chokes performed with the upper and lower extremities, leg and arm locks, sacrifice throws, and much more.

In the book *Progressive Aikido: The Essential Elements*, author Moriteru Ueshiba divides aikido techniques into two main categories: tanren-ho (forging methods) and gi-ho (technical methods). The forging (positional) methods illustrated in this book include suwariwaza, hanmi handachiwaza, tachiwaza, and bukiwaza. The technical methods on display under katamewaza (pinning techniques) are ikkyo, nikyo, sankyo and gokyo; under nagewaza (throwing techniques) are koshinage, iriminage, shihonage and tenbinnage; under nage katamewaza (throw-and-pin techniques) is kotegaeshi. In addition, Andrade-Shihan demonstrates the above discussed forging and technical methods as well as an abundant variety of aikido fundamentals. This presentation also covers correct stance, shikko, aiki ma-ai, aikidome, kuzushi, breakfalls, irimi (omote/ura), tenkan, ushirowaza, atemiwaza, kaeshiwaza and henkawaza. These are also demonstrated within the parameters of our aiki-newaza in the forthcoming techniques.

Each scenario is illustrated with sequential photographs of selected movements and techniques. For each, a **Featured Moment** highlights a particular moment or technique chosen from the scenario for further discussion. To see the complete scenarios unfold in continuous action, refer to the companion DVD where each one may be viewed at normal speed and in slow motion for instructional purposes.

This book has presented the reader with the basic positions and concepts of fundamental aiki-newaza. Each scenario will apply these basics in a variety of ways in accordance with the principles of aikido. It is our hope that this book will inspire sensei to teach aiki newaza and interest students in exploring the martial possibilities provided by newaza training.

THE BRIDGE

At some time, when stepping onto a bridge, you may find yourself in a nether world between life and death. The bridge is the reality of the present moment during which you may confront the heart of conflict face-to-face. The quality of this moment determines victory or defeat. You are faced with survival.

The assailant has approached with an unalterable purpose in mind, distance is closed and a clinch ensues. Willing or not, combat has begun. The assailant tightly wraps his right arm around your back, his left hand grabs your right arm, and he moves his right hip closer to your right hip. For self-protection, you grab the assailant's left side of the neck with your left hand; your right hand grabs his left shoulder.

Putting his martial knowledge to use, the assailant pulls forward and executes a floating hip throw. A hard impact onto the planks of the wooden bridge is imminent. Your calmness and clarity have enabled you to respond so as to lessen the force of the impact.

With this immediate goal in mind, you land with the plantar aspect of the feet first to avoid an injury to your spine. Your buttocks contact the bridge softly, and you lay supine. Your problem is not resolved as the assailant is in a dominant position. Immediately, you slap the left side of his face with your left hand. You know that the atemi will not hurt him, but you do hope to distract him long enough to change the situation in your favor. Along with the face slap, you raise your left leg in preparation for breaking his balance (kuzushi) and throwing him flat on his back.

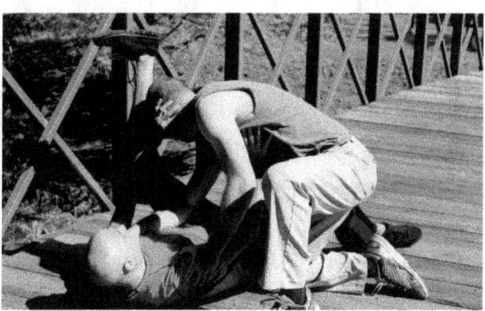

You were able to wrap your leg around the assailant's head and throw him on his back to execute a reversal. For better control, you cover the assailant's face with your left leg, obstructing his vision. Your right foot is anchored next to his right hip. The assailant has made a tactical error by exposing his right arm. Seizing the opportunity, you grab his distal right forearm with both hands, slide your hips very close and tight under his right shoulder, then pull his outstretched arm. Leaning back/down, you raise your hips, creating a fulcrum under his arm. This causes pain in his right elbow as pressure is being applied against the normal range of motion. The assailant knows that he is in danger of having his elbow broken from your application of a right cross-body armlock (juji gatame). In fear and near panic, the assailant taps out in hope of being released from the armlock.

Deciding against brutally breaking the assailant's elbow, you switch the technique (henkawaza) to finish with a bent arm and wristlock. This technique more securely immobilizes an opponent and causes great pain, while being less injurious. You bend the assailant's right arm at the elbow and flex his right wrist to a ninety-degree angle. To secure the wristlock, you place your right hand palm over his bent right dorsal hand and pull the hand inward. At the same time, your left hand grabs your right wrist.

The armlock alone may not be sufficiently motivating to induce full compliance from the assailant. You further motivate him by shifting your hips to the left, closer to his head. This allows you to strike the assailant's groin area with your right heel.

Featured Moment

Not all tactical encounters will unfold as expected. Sometimes the assailant may have martial skills of his own that make him a worthy opponent. When confronted with unavoidable physical conflict, never underestimate the assailant. Do not assume that just because you have studied aikido, jujutsu, karate-do or any other martial art, you are invincible. Over-confidence to the point of cockiness sets you up for a big fall, literally. In this scenario, the assailant executed a takedown and assumed a dominant position from which he could have dispatched you quickly. Calmness, clarity and a thorough understanding of aiki newaza allowed you to take a dire circumstance and turn it into a positive situation in which you can gain control and prevail.

SACRIFICE

During a game of chess, there may come a time when you must sacrifice a lesser piece to achieve the greater goal of survival and victory. You might allow a pawn, a knight, or a bishop to be removed from the board of play to get a check and a following checkmate against the opponent. This same strategy may apply during a physical confrontation. In this scenario, the attacker opens with a left jab. When you deflect the punch with your right hand, the attacker counters with a right punch. You quickly move outside (ura) of the punch and deflect it with your right hand.

The attacker appears to be a formidable striker, so you decide it is in your best interest to take him to the ground. This is not an easy task against a fighter who can continuously rain down blows upon you. Sacrificing your safety in order to improve the tactical situation seems to you a desirable course of action. So you wrap your left hand around his mandible, and rotate his neck as you jump into a scissors with your left leg in front of the attacker's upper torso and your right leg behind his right leg. The attacker attempts to gain control, but he loses balance and falls backward.

This is the moment of sacrifice. The attacker falls backward to the ground taking you down with him. While the attacker takes the brunt of the fall, you also must protect yourself with a breakfall. You have sacrificed your safety and control of the situation in order to gain an advantage. The attacker cannot, at least for the moment, strike at you and he lies on the ground momentarily stunned.

In that moment of incapacitation, you move to mount your attacker. Your sacrifice is about to produce reward.

The attacker's head and left arm become trapped with the right leg as you work to position yourself into a top mount. You rest your left knee on the ground and against his body to stabilize the mount. The attacker's right arm becomes trapped between your abdomen and your right arm as you grab the back of his head.

Now you sit upright to complete a high-top mount. You are seated on the attacker's neck and upper torso; You pull on his extended right arm to create an armbar. You finish your attacker by constricting your hips and lower extremities on both sides of his neck to execute a carotid artery choke. You compress his trachea in a windpipe choke. With your free right arm, you can strike his exposed head. Checkmate!

Featured Moment

In any confrontation, you must be able to quickly and accurately assess the opponent's strengths and weaknesses. You must also know your own capabilities. In this scenario, a long, standup fight was not to your advantage. Your advanced knowledge and abilities in newaza with your merely adequate striking skills necessitated that this confrontation end on the ground. The manner in which you transition from tachiwaza to newaza is crucial. Sometimes, you may have to sacrifice your safety, risking potential injury, in order to achieve the overall goal. The scissor throw is such a sacrifice. You risk a fall onto a hard surface and entanglement with the attacker. The risk is great, but with proper execution and superb agility, the reward may be greater.

You may have learned to live in the moment, letting your movements and techniques arise spontaneously without preplanning. However, this approach can be a source of misunderstanding and have dire consequences for your strategic success. Like the game of chess, you may have to plan your defense several moves ahead to set up an opponent for eventual defeat. This skill is the hallmark of professional fighting, be it MMA, wrestling or boxing. Realize that any conscious planning with its lightning-fast execution by the body-mind always happens in the present moment. Use all of your intelligence, conscious and unconscious, to checkmate your opponent.

Hanmi Handachi/Suwariwaza Surprise

In suwariwaza and hanmi handachiwaza, we presented several examples of these traditional aikido techniques in a dojo setting. Most aikido schools that instruct in these techniques do so more as a bow to aikido tradition than as a practical form of self-defense. Now, revisit this form of ground fighting in a real-world, extreme scenario.

A chance encounter with a gang member in a once peaceful park turns ugly. You may have trespassed on a gang-controlled territory, or he may just be looking for a fight. The gang member approaches you wearing a stone-cold countenance, unleashes a wicked left jab that misses and immediately follows up with a right spinning back fist strike that you deflect.

As you retreat, the sizable gang member moves forward and gives a mighty two-handed push to your midsection.

His shove sends you reeling backward. Remembering your most basic aikido training, you perform a back roll (ukemi). You will finish the ukemi in seiza.

The gang member is not yet finished with you. He closes the distance quickly. As he comes within tactical range, inspiration arises and you rise up on one knee to deliver a rapid front snap kick to his lower abdomen, giving it all you have within you.

The gang member rolls backward in pain.

Clearly affected by the low blow to the lower abdomen, he rises only to his knees (suwariwaza). You knee walk (shikko) closer to him and he throws an overhead strike (shomenuchi). You deflect the half-hearted strike with your left hand and grab his right wrist.

You stand up and move alongside the gang member (hanmi handachiwaza) so that your center (hara) is directed at him and his center points away. You know that this is an inherently stronger position. With your right hand, you perform a finger sankyo and drive him onto his back.

Now on his back, the gang member grabs your left wrist. You release the finger sankyo and box his ear. Your wide stance and lowered center help you maintain your stability and make it more difficult for him to break free.

You prepare to finish him by hooking your right arm under his right axilla and pressing that arm against the right side of his neck. You slip your left arm around the left side of his neck and grab his right wrist for a choke wrap. To secure a very tight choke you raise him up slightly and let him down. You step over the gang member's abdomen while keeping a tight choke.

Finally, you sit back onto the ground, maintain a tight choke wrap and deliver several right heel strikes to his lower abdomen and/or his exposed groin. The use of the choke wrap technique allows you to immobilize the gang member. The right heel strikes to his injured groin area would make him unable to continue the fight. You could now release him and exit the area before any fellow gang members appeared. Unfortunately, you will have to find other parks to enjoy.

Featured Moment

The element of surprise is crucial to any tactical situation. It can be all that separates victory from defeat. The Japanese surprise attack on the American naval base at Pearl Harbor, Hawaii, is a classic example of the advantage of surprise. American naval ships moored in the docks were sunk by waves of undetected torpedo-carrying airplanes. The element of surprise is effective, no matter the scale of a confrontation.

In this scenario, after being pushed backward, you sat in seiza as the gang member rushed toward you (hanmi handachi). This fellow was larger and probably stronger than you. He probably had more street fights under his belt than you would ever have or want. Clearly, appearances indicated that he had every reason to believe that he would prevail. What you had in your favor was guile and the element of surprise. Why would he expect the delivery of a front snap kick from a sitting position having sufficient force to injure? From the moment that kick struck its target, the fight was effectively over for the gangbanger. Your skill in newaza would be all that was needed to finish the opponent.

ATEMIWAZA

This scenario demonstrates the value of atemi in placing a foe on the defensive. Continued well-timed, and effectively targeted strikes can make it extremely difficult for your foe to regain his initiative. While forced to cover up against your atemi, you are left free to finish him with newaza.

The foe moves toward you and throws a left open-hand strike as a distraction for his next planned move. You redirect his strike with your opposing hand.

Continuing to move forward, your foe dives low and attempts to "shoot" your left leg for a single leg takedown. Reacting quickly, you push his neck and head toward the ground. Your foe grabs at your left leg but fails to upend you.

His unsuccessful attempt at a takedown makes his eventual downfall all but certain. Your foe is in a perilous tactical position, being face down with the back of his head exposed and unable to defend himself. You take advantage of his weak position to deliver two punches to the back of his head. Your foe must cover his head to prevent damage from any further strikes. He remains immobile, but he still holds your left ankle.

You tenkan (body turn), straddle your foe and deliver an elbow strike to his side. You stay very close to his back behind him (shikaku) and deliver several more elbow strikes to his rib area. Your foe's continued hold on your left ankle is becoming a real liability for him. By grabbing the ankle, he keeps your leg close to his neck and facilitates an eventual choke.

In an attempt to roll your foe, you grab his right arm with both hands and begin to rise and sit down on his back. By releasing one arm and then grabbing again, you can continue to strike his side. He still maintains a hold on your left ankle, though that hold is weakening.

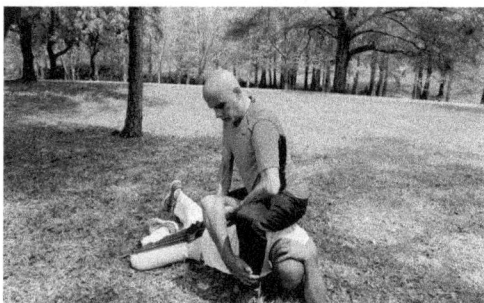

To complete the side rollover of your foe, you begin to sit back down as you hold his right arm. Lying down on your back, you outstretch his right arm for a right cross body armlock. At the same time, you wrap your left leg around his neck and lock it with your right leg to secure a side triangle choke.

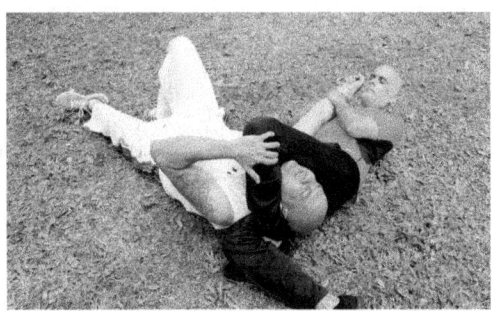

Featured Moment

This scenario turned in your favor early on when you avoided being taken down with your foe's attempted single leg takedown. From that moment on your foe was in a defenseless position by having his back turned toward you. It allowed you to use atemi to occupy his attention, inflict pain and control the tactical situation. Atemi do not need to be knockout strikes in order to be effective. Distraction is oftentimes sufficient to get the desired result.

Knife Disarm

You collect your mail at the mailbox, turn to leave, and are confronted by a knife-wielding thug. As he approaches, you back away and maintain a safe separation. Determined to carry out his knife attack, he slashes downward and then upward without connecting. On his third downward slash, you move to the outside and intercept the strike with your left forearm. Your lifeline faces away from the knife blade in order to maximize protection of your vital organs.

Maintaining a "sticky" connection to the thug's knife arm with your left forearm, you grab the top of the thug's right wrist (knife hand) with your right hand. You enter to the front (omote) and intend to perform an ikkyo takedown.

To perform an ikkyo, you redirect the thug's right arm upward in a circular arc. You place your left hand against his right elbow for leverage. Unexpectedly, the thug grabs the front of your shirt with his left hand. This seemingly insignificant action will alter the entire course of this tactical scenario.

The ikkyo in progress and the thug's grab of your shirt unbalances (kuzushi) him. He falls onto his back, bringing you down with him. At this point, the ikkyo is no longer an option. This is a moment fraught with danger. The thug still holds the knife pointed in your direction, and you have not established a controlling technique. Most anything could happen, some things for your good, and other things, not so much. Whoever possesses the quickest and most flexible mind, one that can envision a wide range of possibilities and make immediate choices in the present moment, stands the best chance of surviving this potentially lethal encounter.

As you are brought down, you control his knife arm by changing the position of your right hand and tightly gripping his right wrist and bent right elbow for a right bent armlock (ude garami). His right shoulder is immobilized, so he cannot strike at you with the knife. You momentarily release your left hand and deliver a strike to the thug's head.

The thug has dragged you down on top of him into a half-top mount position. Seizing the moment and taking full advantage of your superior position, you attempt to disarm him of the knife. You begin by slipping your left arm under his bent right elbow and grab his right wrist with your right hand. Your left hand grabs your right forearm to secure this lock. The thug's forearm is angled upward and perpendicular to the ground. His right knife hand rests palm up on the ground at an angle perpendicular to his forearm. You tip your left elbow upward, forcing the thug to drop the knife.

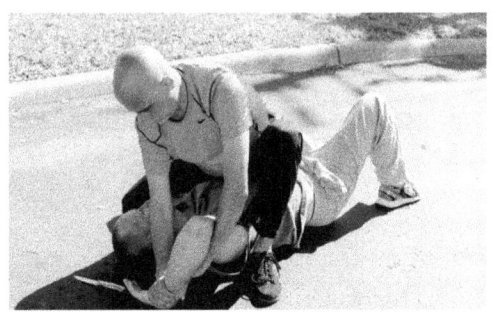

Now that the thug is without a weapon and has lost confidence, you slowly loosen and release the bent armlock and strike his right temple with your elbow. Then you pick up the knife from the ground and escape with a left forward ukemi. You rise to a standing position wielding the knife in your right hand. The situation is reversed. The thug wisely decides to retreat and live to fight another day.

Featured Moment

During a tactical situation against an armed opponent should you disarm him? Some martial artists will insist that disarming the opponent must come first. This is certainly desirable if the flow of the encounter allows for this tactic. Had you been able to complete the ikkyo technique, you could have applied a nikyo pin to disarm him as soon as he was brought down on one knee. Events are often unpredictable. In this scenario, the disarm technique had to be delayed until you had regained full control of the thug. The important point is that any disarm technique must be done from a dominant, secure position. There is no room for error. You must succeed on the first try.

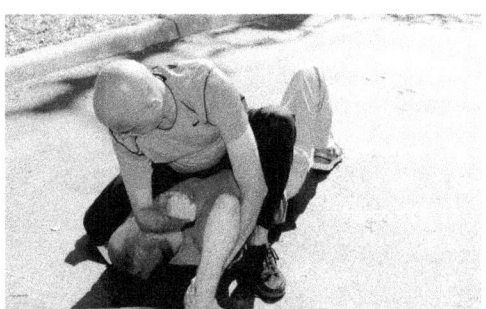

ON YOUR BACK

In today's world, the workplace is no stranger to violence. In front of your clinic, a presumably disgruntled and aggressive patient approaches you and throws a high front kick that narrowly misses your head.

Standing alongside and facing the aggressor, you counter with a slap to his face. The aggressor deftly evades your strike.

The two of you stand in close proximity and enter a clinch. The aggressor, an MMA enthusiast, quickly wraps his hands under your legs and pulls hard, executing a double-leg takedown.

You lose your balance and fall to the pavement, landing on your back with no time to perform a breakfall. Instead, you hold onto the back of the aggressor's neck to avoid injury and "having the wind knocked out of you." You have the aggressor in the open guard position.

You reposition yourself by moving your body to the left and resting on your side. A struggle ensues over control of the aggressor's right arm. You seek to grab and control the arm while he desperately tries to prevent the likely outcome should you succeed.

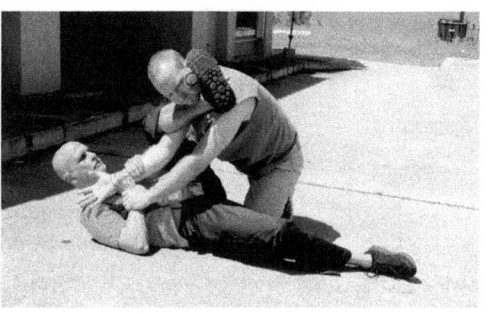

Having secured the aggressor's right arm, you swing your left leg over the right side of his neck and pull on his outstretched arm for a right side armbar.

Featured Moment

As many MMA contestants have repeatedly demonstrated, the double leg takedown is an effective technique for taking someone to the ground. An aikidoka facing an altercation should not assume that being taken down, even by a trained fighter couldn't occur. In any tactical scenario, there is no guarantee that you will remain upright. Should you go down, positioning yourself in a mount or any other advantageous position may be difficult.

With extensive experience in newaza, you will have learned to view the guard as an advantageous position from which to defend yourself. A variety of chokes, pressure points, armbars and wristlocks are available for use from the guard. It is even possible to evade and deflect strikes to the head. Always enter any violent encounter with shoshin, a beginner's mind. Be open and responsive to any and all possibilities that may unfold in the course of the action.

MORE DEFENSES FROM THE GUARD

It is usually not a good idea to frequent publically recognized high-crime areas. So it should not surprise you that, when passing through such a location, someone looking for a fight accosts you. This fighter wastes no effort on misguided strikes and immediately bends low to attempt a double leg takedown.

The fighter wraps his hands under your legs, pulls and drives you down onto the pavement, flat on your back. You protect yourself from injury by holding onto the fighter's arm and back.

You have the fighter in the open guard position. He attempts a bent armlock (ude garami). You counter by striking several times to his neck, with your left-hand blade.

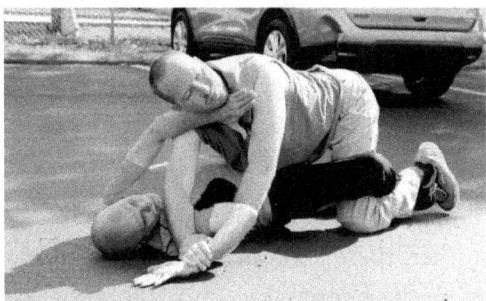

Before the fighter secures the ude garami, you grab and lower his head with your left hand as you begin to wrap your left leg around his neck.

Realizing that he has lost the initiative, the fighter releases the bent arm lock while still applying pressure on your right shoulder. You have wrapped your left leg around the fighter's neck. With your now free right hand, you grab your left ankle. You also slip your left hand under his neck and grab your left ankle to create a choke.

You release the right-hand grab of your left ankle. With your now-free right hand; you push the right side of the fighter's face.

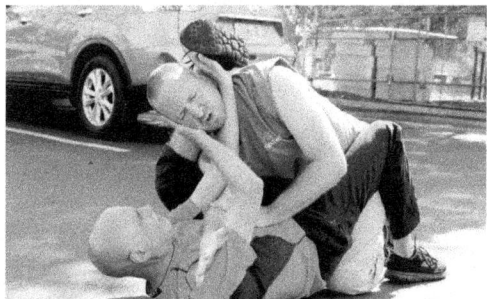

In preparation for changing technique, you throw the fighter to the left, roll him over and release the choke you had with your leg. When you are moving out of one technique and into another, there is no break in the motion. You flow into the next technique without leaving the fighter any time to mount a counter.

With your left leg over the fighter's neck and your right leg placed over his abdomen, you grab his right wrist and outstretch his arm to finish with a right cross-body armbar.

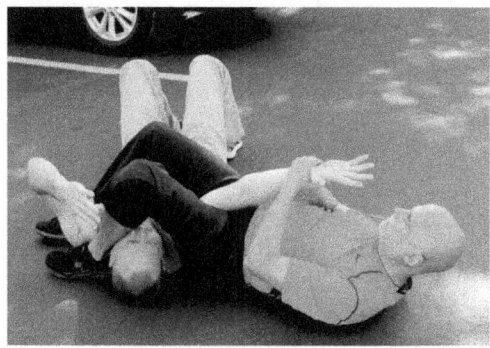

Featured Moment

So why change techniques during the course of the encounter? You had a secure choke on the fighter but gave it up for an armbar. Why? There are many reasons why such a change might be warranted. Each person will have his or her own reasons for the choice of finishing technique.

A complex choke like the one illustrated may require too much strength and endurance to successfully complete. Also, you do not want the fighter on top of you, should he break free of the choke. In addition, if the choke is completed, then how do you determine its effect on the fighter? If he is unconscious, how long will he remain in that condition—long enough for you to escape? A more ethical consideration involves how much harm you ought to inflict. A choke can directly kill; it can also kill indirectly by dislodging plaque in the arteries. Does this mean you should never employ a choke on an opponent? No! Each tactical encounter is different. Your abilities must be weighed against the dangerousness of the opponent. Your chance to survive the fight is the ultimate determiner of your actions.

The armbar is a simpler and easier technique to employ. It is highly effective in immobilizing the opponent. When performing an armbar, you have the choice of whether to seek submission or incapacitate the opponent by breaking the elbow. An elbow break will certainly harm the fighter but will not threaten his life. If the fighter has learned to fear you, then letting him off with a warning (submission) may be sufficient punishment. Again, opponents and the options used against them will vary.

REAR NAKED CHOKE

Walking out the back door of your dojo where you have taught an aikido class on newaza, you notice someone lurking nearby. As it turns out, this antagonist believes he is a superior martial artist and is determined to prove himself right by taking on a worthy opponent. He approaches and initiates a skirmish by throwing a right hook. You move to the outside and land a right atemi to his liver. At the same time, you deflect the hook punch with your left unbendable arm in a kind of up-and-in parrying motion while keeping connected to the attack.

Quickly, you move behind the antagonist and begin to slip your right arm around his neck, just under the chin.

For a moment or two, you rise onto your tiptoes in preparation to rapidly secure a rear mount naked choke. Your right arm wraps around the antagonist's neck, and you grasp your left bicep muscle with your right hand.

To unbalance the antagonist (kuzushi), you lower your center (hara) and bring him to the ground in an upright sitting position. You tighten the choke by pushing the back of his head with your left hand while you squeeze your right arm even more tightly against his carotid arteries.

You finish the technique by rolling back so that he lies face up on top of you (rear mount). Hooking him with your legs prevents him from bridging and rolling away. Once he is unconscious, you release him and exit the area.

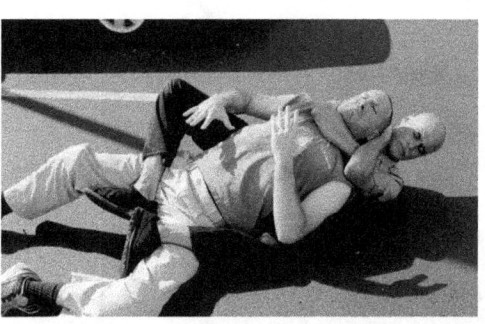

Featured Moment

Traditional aikido instruction for the advanced student covers attacks from behind (ushiro-waza) and escapes from certain chokes (kubi shime-waza) in order to develop a sixth sense about a partner's position. In this scenario, the attacker does not move behind in order to grab or choke; rather, you move behind the attacker in order to apply a rear naked choke. The rear naked choke is very rarely performed in aikido. This particular choke is very effective at rendering an opponent unconscious and is very difficult to counter. Kubishime, as taught in aikido, is impractical on the street because it is nearly impossible to secure a strong choke without using two hands. The rear naked choke is the premier shime-waza taught in Mukei No Ryu aikido.

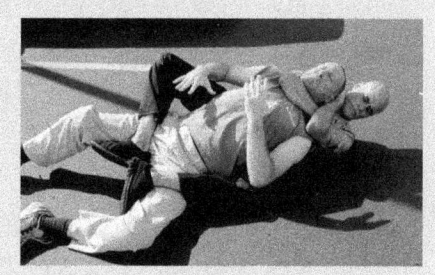

SIDE TRIANGLE CHOKE

Walking in an isolated area, a mugger sees what he believes to be an easy target. He approaches and throws a right hook punch. You intercept the strike.

You attempt a four-corner throw (shihonage).

The mugger manages to escape the shihonage and resumes his attack.

The mugger executes a double leg takedown (described in previous scenarios).

While holding onto the mugger, you fall on your back and break the fall with your upper extremity.

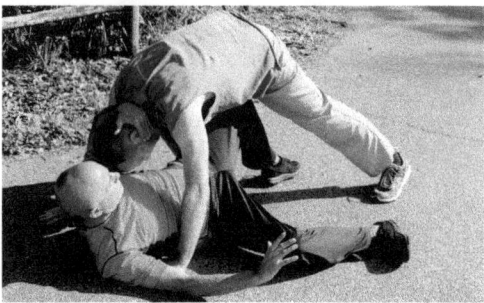

The mugger moves into a cross mount.

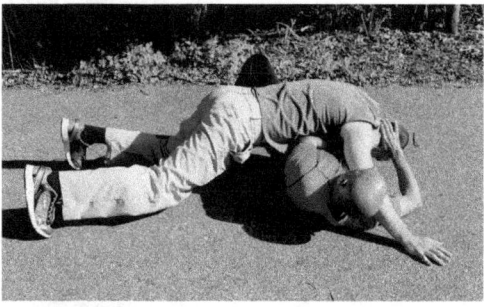

Before the mugger can either secure your appendages or move into another more advantageous position, you grab the back of his neck to control his head and raise your legs toward his head.

You wrap your right leg behind the back of his neck and lock the right leg just above the ankle with your left leg for a side triangle choke. You strike several times to his right rib area.

Featured Moment

For most martial techniques, including those of aikido, there are reversal techniques that allow the opponent to counteract and escape immobilization. Once this is accomplished, the opponent can reposition himself, flee to safety, or continue with the attack. In this scenario, the mugger escaped the shihonage and immediately resumed his attack by executing a double leg takedown. While carrying out a technique, there is often a brief moment of vulnerability. If his timing is right, the attacker may take advantage of a weakness inherent in the technique itself or of a fault in your application of the technique. If your application of a technique is weak, that is a problem that can be corrected by your martial arts instructor. If the technique itself can be broken, then you must become aware of its strengths and weaknesses. As demonstrated in this scenario, if the opponent counters your initial technique, you will have an opportunity to recover and favorably change the dynamic of the encounter. Most importantly, stay calm and focused. Take full advantage of anything the environment offers and counter his next move with a finishing technique of your own.

BABY-SNATCHER

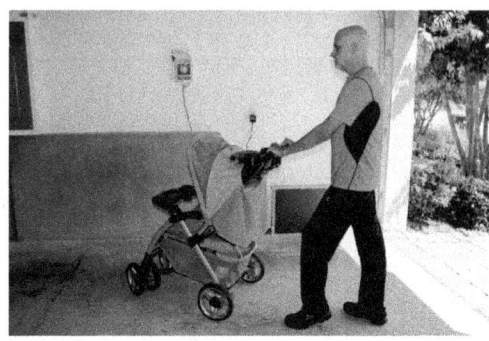

Returning from a walk with the baby in a stroller, you enter the garage and prepare to take the baby inside. Suddenly a baby snatcher enters the still-open garage. Hoping to scare him away, you grab a baby bottle and throw it at the snatcher. Undeterred, he picks up a plastic lawn chair to use as a weapon against you. You grab an empty gallon milk jug to defend yourself. The baby snatcher swings the chair at you, and you deflect the strike with the milk jug.

In that process, you both lose your weapons. You slap his face with your right hand and follow up with a downward, right elbow strike to the left side of his face.

The baby snatcher begins to fall but quickly recovers and does a double leg takedown.

He sits in the top mount position. He tries to wrap his right arm around the back of your head and grasps his right hand with his left hand in a square grip to create a choke. Meanwhile, you have wrapped your right arm around the back of his neck. Stalemate!

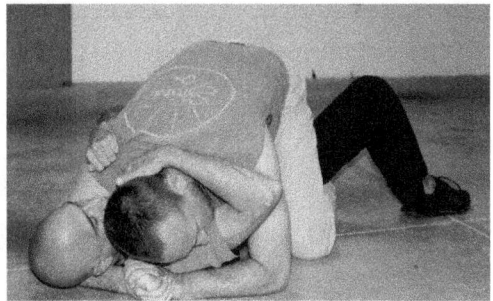

You wriggle back and forth, trying to unbalance him. Finally, you touch the back of his neck with your left hand to trap his right arm and arch your back (bridge) to take his balance. With your right hand pushing the left side of the baby snatcher's face, you roll him to the left and off of you.

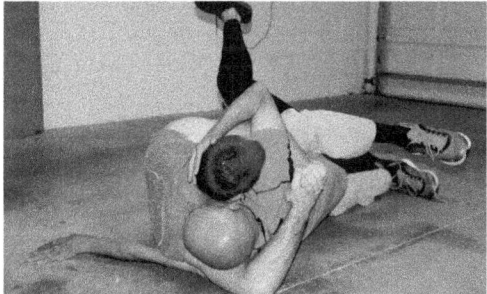

The baby snatcher's right hand grabs the back of your neck, while lying on his back and has you in the open guard (legs unlocked). You trap his right arm and simultaneously apply sankyo to his left hand.

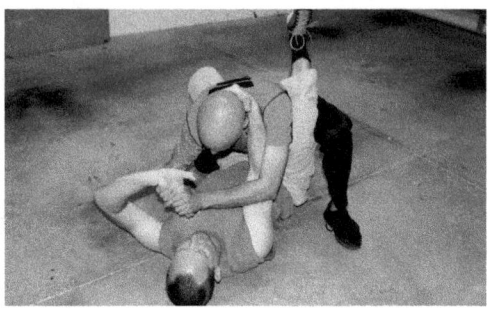

You slap the right side of his face to distract him from the sankyo you apply to his left hand. The pain from the sankyo keeps him from closing the guard. His right hand secures your neck to prevent you from getting up.

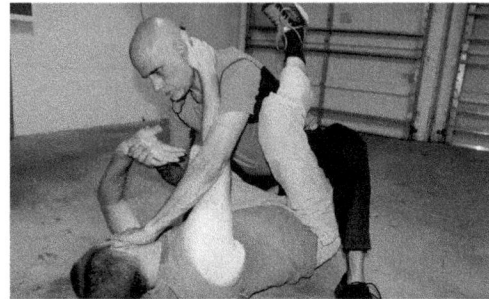

You release the sankyo and slap him in the face again in preparation for a nikyo.

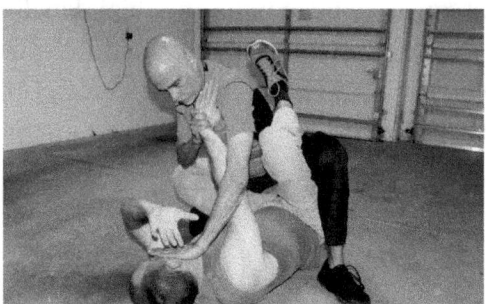

You grab the baby snatcher's right hand and forearm to apply nikyo.

To prepare for your finishing technique, you push his right leg away with your left hand and secure it with your left knee pressed against his inner thigh to pass the guard. You apply a one-handed nikyo to his right wrist to maintain pain compliance.

You release the nikyo, turn and cradle his left leg in your right arm in order to outstretch his leg.

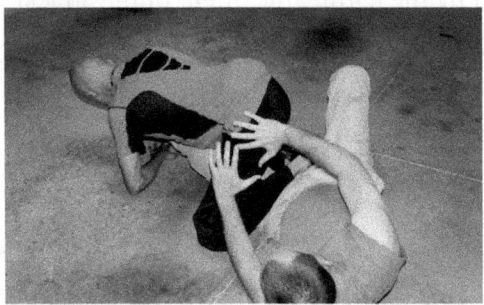

While holding his left leg, you begin to roll underneath this leg. You wrap your right leg over his left leg and hook your right ankle under his right leg. This action, along with pressure from your hips against his left leg, acts as a fulcrum to hyperextend this leg to create a straight left knee lock. You apply enough pressure to cripple him and thereby prevent him from snatching your baby.

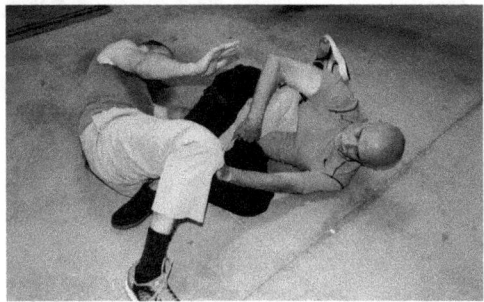

Featured Moment

While self-defense may be considered acceptable in order to save your own life, it is noble to save the life of a threatened family member or the life of anyone who is incapable of defending oneself. We not only possess an instinct for self-preservation, but also an instinct to defend our families from harm. Without such instincts, the human species could not have survived. In this scenario, the progression of the encounter moved from an attempt to deter the baby snatcher from fulfilling his goal, to immobilizing him with various strikes and wrist locks (sankyo and nikyo), to rendering him incapable of causing harm to the innocent and defenseless baby. While during an act of self-defense, you have the option of allowing the opponent to flee after the altercation has been decided in your favor. This option should not exist when your family is attacked. The opponent must be rendered incapable of continuing by whatever means necessary. The ethical considerations in a confrontation should be determined by the nature, the intent of the attacker and the nature of and relationship to those threatened with harm.

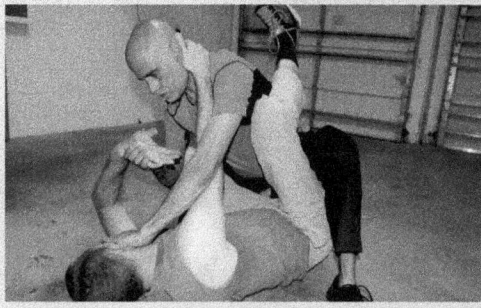

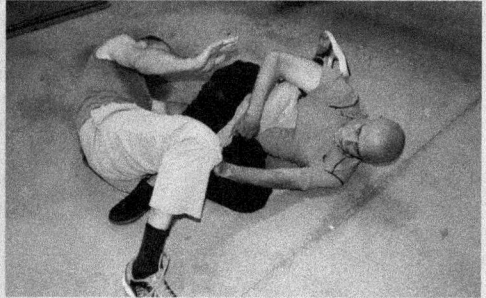

Sen No Sen

Violence can occur before the first overt violent act is committed. The opponent telegraphs his intention to wage a physical conflict. You read his intention correctly and anticipate an imminent attack that you might not be prepared to resist. In an attempt to either dissuade the opponent from attacking or to end the confrontation before the opponent has actualized his violent intent, you throw a high in-to-out kick to his face. Unfortunately, your kick fails to hit the intended target, and the battle is on.

The opponent throws a roundhouse kick, and you catch it before any damage is done.

The opponent pushes you, and you fall backward and down.

You land on your back, and the opponent covers you with a cross mount. Each of you wraps an arm around the other's neck.

The opponent changes from a cross-chest position to a scarf hold (head-and-arm pin).

He wraps his right arm behind your neck. His left hand grabs your right arm closely to the right side of your chest in a tight hold around his body and he spreads his legs for a solid foundation. This makes it difficult for you to breathe as his body shifts toward you (compression). You grab your left wrist with your right hand to trap his left arm and to support your left forearm. You push against his neck with your left forearm to create a separation so as to ease the pressure in preparation for your next move.

You lift your left leg across the opponent's face as you cease pushing with your forearm and release the grip on your wrist.

You work your left leg in front of and against the opponent's neck.

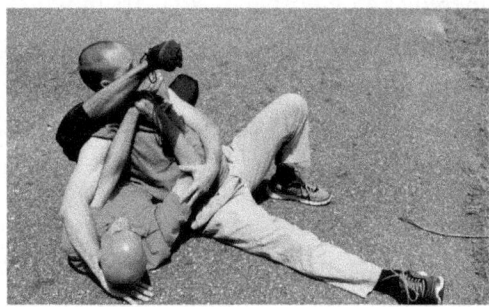

You lift and extend the opponent's left arm. You begin the process to create a triangle choke by locking your left ankle with your folded right leg.

The opponent releases his right arm wrap. You apply a two-handed sankyo to his left wrist and use your left elbow to prevent him from using his free right arm to interfere with the sankyo. Since he is on his back and lying perpendicular across your body, you can use your legs to arch his back and drag his head to the ground for better control. Throughout, the opponent is on top of, but not facing, the defender. The defender is beneath the opponent in the supine position.

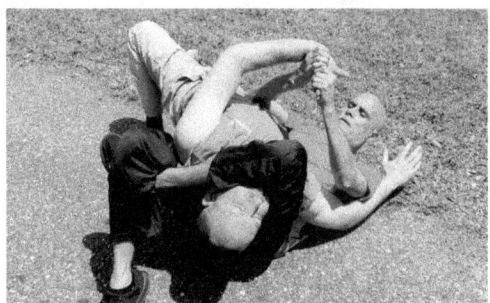

Featured Moment

Aikido is often considered as a defensive martial art in which nage does not initiate physical conflict. While most often this is true, there are exceptions. For example, shomenuchi ikkyo can be performed by nage striking shomenuchi and uke raising an arm to block or deflect the strike. As uke raises his arm in defense; nage grabs the offered arm and applies an ikkyo takedown.

This still does not get at the meaning of sen no sen. Sen no sen involves sensing another person's energy as either friendly or threatening. Once a person's negative intentions are felt and/or observed, an aikidoka can respond as if violence has already commenced; and indeed, on an inner plane, it has occurred. If a hostile is armed, you may have to initiate action to prevent an armed attack. Obviously, you cannot allow someone who you have sensed is dangerous to draw a gun on you. On the other hand, if your action is not effective, then a battle will ensue, and the outcome will be unknown.

While sen no sen should be an element of military combat on a battlefield, law enforcement may not consider hostile intent sufficient provocation to "stand your ground" in a civilian setting. Preemptive strikes carry the risk of being viewed as blatant aggression. Keep in mind, most martial arts techniques were created and refined for use in military campaigns, for protection of cultural institutions, and finally, for self-defense. What is perfectly legal is to use the art of sen no sen to develop your intuitive feelings regarding the intentions of others. Foreknowledge is strength.

THE MORE THE BETTER

Many victims of violence know their attackers. In this scenario, a long-time rival takes advantage of an opportunity to inflict harm. Your rival comes armed with a broken glass bottle. As he stabs at your abdomen, you deflect the strike with your left hand and deliver a right open back-hand strike to his face. As you gain control of his right arm, you lock it with a nikyo, and he drops to one knee.

While maintaining the nikyo, you let your rival rise up off the ground so that you can kick him in the abdomen. He drops the broken bottle.

You regain your wide, stable stance and, holding the nikyo with your right hand, you strike him in the face with a left-hand claw.

With the attacker stunned by your face strike, you tenkan and enter to the rear (ura) and place your right hand in his arm pit, raising his right arm in preparation for a throw.

You turn and go under your rival's elevated right arm and apply an elbow-lock throw (tenbin-nage) using your left shoulder as a fulcrum, while dragging his right arm directly to the ground to throw him.

As your rival falls to the ground, you maintain the hold on his right arm. You launch yourself down and on top of him, pressing your weight against his ribs.

You wrap your left arm around his neck and continue controlling his right arm.

Now you apply sankyo to your rival's right hand. Your left arm wraps around his head with his right arm pressed against his head, forming a headlock.

Grabbing his left hand, you use your left leg to create a bent armlock while maintaining sankyo.

The armlock is secured by locking your left ankle with your right leg. You tighten your control of your rival by compressing your body against his and cranking his neck. You are now applying three techniques simultaneously: sankyo, bent armbar and neck crank. For good measure, you pick up the broken bottle and hold it inches from his face so he can clearly see it, a not-too-subtle message that even your rival should understand.

Featured Moment

Sometimes it is necessary to demoralize an opponent, allowing him no hope of reversal and/or escape. In this scenario, your rival was armed, and you were not. A false sense of confidence drove him to attack. From the first stab with the broken bottle to the finishing techniques, your rival was never in control of the tactical situation. While the bent arm bar or the sankyo were sufficient to subdue him (the neck crank, not so much), applying all three techniques simultaneously created pain in multiple locations of his body and utterly immobilized him. Any hope of prevailing he might have had, you ruthlessly squelched.

SWEPT OFF HIS FEET

Sometimes you may require a more direct method of taking an attacker to the ground than trying to execute a complicated technique. Aside from a double-leg takedown, a strong single-leg sweep may suit your needs. In this scenario, the attacker moves toward you and grabs your left shoulder with his right hand.

He throws a left-hook punch. You redirect his punch, enter and grab both of his arms then proceed to unbalance him (kuzushi).

You sweep the back of his right leg with your right leg and the attacker falls on his back. His grip on your shirt drags you down with him. *Note:* the leg sweep alters the attacker's equilibrium from an unstable "two-pole" stance to a wobbly "one-pole" stance that ensures the attacker topples.

You straddle the attacker in a high half-mount position. You maintain a hold on his right wrist. The attacker attempts a reversal but fails. You place your right hand across his face to distract him and control his head.

You maintain control of both of the attacker's arms. As you extend his left arm and swing it up and across your body, he reaches for and grabs your shirt.

The attacker loses his grip on your shirt as you swing his extended arm to the ground. You trap his left arm on the ground with your right knee.

Focusing on the attacker's right arm that you still control, extend it across his head and touch his right hand to the ground for a straight armlock.

The attacker struggles to roll onto his side, so you end the straight armlock and you apply a very quick nikyo pin to his right wrist.

You release the nikyo pin and atemi to his face with your right hand. Then you manipulate his right arm and wrist to apply a gokyo pin. After you deem sufficient pain has been applied, you exit the scene with a forward left ukemi, leaving the attacker writhing in pain. Maintaining total awareness, you turn to face and observe the attacker.

Featured Moment

Although not often taught in aikido (Mukei No Ryu aikido being one exception), the leg sweep is one of the most effective takedown techniques. As in this scenario, a leg sweep can be applied in conjunction with irimi-nage (entering technique). With your right unbendable arm, you can either grab the attacker's left arm to help control his body, or you can strike his upper chest and neck area from low to high accompanying the leg sweep. There are many styles of leg sweeping used in different martial arts. They are fun and effective. Learn them all!

165

PRIVATE PROPERTY PROTECTION

In the United States of America, you have the right not only to protect yourself from physical harm at the hands of another, but also to protect your property from the threat of damage and/or theft. In this scenario, you encounter a metal pipe-wielding thief who, when discovered and warned about his infringement of your property rights, initiates an attack.

Once the thief raises the pipe in a menacing fashion, you know that self-defense is a necessity. The thief attempts a right overhead strike with the metal pipe. You enter diagonally left and catch his right arm with your unbendable, left arm for an aikidome. You strike his abdomen with your right fist.

The thief drops the pipe and you maintain aikidome, or a movement to change the trajectory of an attack, as you raise your right arm and lock his bent right arm. You try to unbalance him, but he regains his upright posture.

You wrap your left hand behind the thief's head.

The thief counters by grabbing your head with both hands in a frontal neck clinch and begins to pull your head down. The thief delivers a right-knee kick as you simultaneously throw two right punches to his lower abdomen and deflect the kick with your left hand.

The thief maintains the clinch. You lower your center and place your right hand against his left upper arm.

You rise up, keeping your right hand against his left shoulder and push him downward, striking with your left fist to his mid-section and ducking under to extricate yourself from the clinch. The thief is bent forward at the waist.

Standing alongside the thief, you rest your right hand against his lower back and quickly raise your left unbendable arm to strike him in the neck (iriminage).

As the thief falls down, you lock your arms around his neck (head lock), step forward with your rear leg and go to the ground with him. You slide your left leg forward, as if sliding into a base in the game of baseball, to increase your stability.

You reach for and grab the metal pipe with your right hand while you maintain the headlock with your left arm. You drop the pipe out of the thief's reach. Now you change the headlock to a basic square grip in which you clasp both hands together and jam his head to create additional pressure on his neck (side naked square lock).

The left arm and forearm squeeze both sides of the thief's neck as you release your right arm so as to grasp your right bicep with your left hand and place your right hand against the top of his head for naked choke from the side.

Because this thief has been resistant to chokes, you release the grip on his head to grab the metal pipe to apply a stronger choke. You grasp one end of the pipe in your left hand. You rest the pipe against the left side of his neck and grasp the other end with your right hand then squeeze. Using the pipe as a part of the side naked choke increases the pressure against the thief's left carotid artery. At this point, the thief should be unconscious. You have protected your property.

Featured Moment

In this scenario, you are threatened with a weapon, held in a frontal neck clinch, and knee kicked. What unfolds is unplanned and chaotic. Yet, within the apparent disorder, a kind of order emerges. Like many sporting competitions, there is an ebb and flow in the action in which, first one, then the other prevails. This scenario demonstrates the futility of trying to plan your every move throughout a physical confrontation. The only viable choice you have is to rely on your training for your skill set, react in the moment with an unobstructed mind to whatever is presented, and allow your body-mind to create the actions like an inspired painter with a new canvas.

Only when you have the thief in a headlock and then a choke, do you engage your intellectual and moral faculties. For now, you have choices to make, choices that must be made under the full light of reason. How far do you take the choke? Do you simply apply pain and expect compliance? Do you render the thief unconscious? Or, do you kill? Whichever course of action you choose, consequences will follow. Switching between these modes of consciousness must be near instantaneous. Your study of aikido (and other martial arts) should prepare you for acting in the moment (Zen) as well as help you to weigh actions and effects in an ethical manner grounded in the life force (Morihei Ueshiba).

Home Invasion

A home invasion is one of the most dangerous and traumatic assaults one can face. The invasion can occur any time, day or night. You may be armed or unarmed; most likely, the invader will be armed. While robbery is usually the motive, the invader may intend to kill you and your family in order to eliminate witnesses, or he may kill all of you just for the thrill it provides.

In this scenario, the home invader strikes just before you enter your home. With gun drawn, he forces you inside. You have only moments to decide whether you will risk your life in self-defense or whether you will obey the commands of the invader in hopes that he will spare your life. Since the law recognizes that "your home is your castle," and the armed invader has entered your home with the intent to do harm, you are within your rights to use whatever means are available to defend yourself. How you respond to this assault should be determined by your state of mind, your skill in firearm counter techniques, your position vis-à-vis the invader, the possibility of collateral damage, and your assessment of the psychological state of the invader. The authors of this book cannot recommend any specific course of action should such a situation really occur. This scenario does present one possible means of self-defense against such an attack.

On a day like any other, you pull into the driveway, exit your car, and approach the front door to your home. Suddenly, you find yourself with a gun held to the back of your head. The home invader orders you to unlock the door and enter your residence. At this point, you comply with his demands. You understand that you must remain calm and begin assessing the tactical situation moment by moment. The invader has his left hand resting on your left shoulder, and the gun, in his right hand, is pressed against the back of your head. He walks you into the living room and lowers the gun from your head to your lower back while maintaining his left hand on your shoulder. You decide that the moment for resistance is at hand, and you raise your left arm as a distraction and in preparation for what is to come.

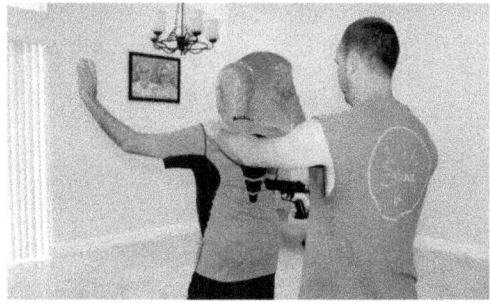

You quickly turn to the right and deflect the gun away from your body.

As you complete about 180 degrees of your turn, you strike the invader with your left elbow. As you cradle his right wrist in your right arm, your left arm reaches for his right wrist.

You gain control of his gun hand by grasping his right wrist with both hands and proceed to apply a kotegaeshi to take the invader to the floor. The invader falls onto his back. The gun points away from you and somewhat toward the invader. He grabs your right forearm with his left hand, and you strike to his face with your left hand.

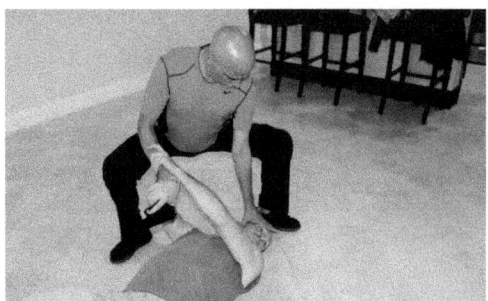

You rise up and break his grip on your arm. As the invader begins to get up, you begin to move behind him. You raise his gun arm, keep the gun directed away, and wrap your right hand around the left side of his face as he sits upright.

You continue to turn until you are close behind him. Then you throw your left leg around his upper torso followed by the right leg in an attempt to form a triangle choke. Then using both legs, he is brought down simultaneously controlling his head tight to the abdomen and controlling the hand holding the gun for an armlock.

Your right leg rises and then descends to lock your left ankle securely to form a triangle. From this position, you can squeeze your legs together tightly to constrict his neck and chest to make breathing difficult. You still maintain control of his gun hand.

Now you disarm him by applying a one-handed straight armbar. The invader drops the gun. You release the hold, but not his right wrist, in order to roll onto your side just long enough to secure the gun. Then you point the gun at the invader's head. You have finished with a rear triangular choke and arm lock.

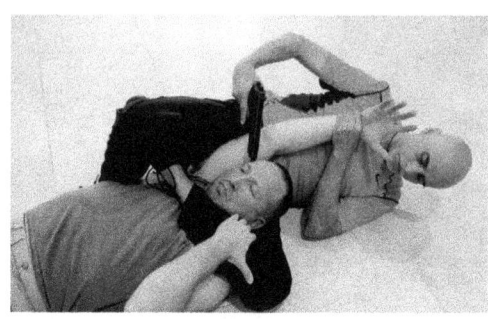

Featured Moment

When should one apply a disarm technique during an assault with a firearm? Some would insist this occur at the earliest moment possible. Others would delay disarming until after the assailant has been neutralized and secured. This is a common debate among martial artists. There is no one right answer. Each situation presents its own opportunities. The only potential problem with attempting to disarm an assailant before he is fully under your control is that, if you are not successful, you will likely be shot. On the other hand, the longer you must attempt to maintain control over his gun hand, the more opportunities you will have to lose such control, in which case, you will likely be shot. In other words, success is everything. There are no points for second place, only a visit to a hospital and/or a morgue. So, train diligently!

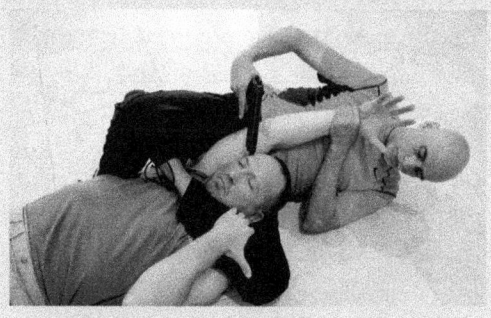

Concluding Thoughts:
A Call to Shugyo

We can honor the martial visions and wisdom of the samurai, Morihei Ueshiba, Jigoro Kano, and other martial art pioneers by returning to the values that made the artists and their creations great. Martial arts were their passion, vocation, and life. Each worked relentlessly to perfect their techniques and build their spirits. There were no shortcuts! Modern martial artists owe the past masters respect for their accomplishments and should desire to follow in their footsteps to whatever degree possible. For the aikidoka, he or she should demonstrate the same open mind, flexibility, and creativity of Ueshiba and Kano and make newaza an accepted and vital part of aikido curriculum. We of Mukei No Ryu aikido have taken this task to heart and strive to translate spiritual philosophy into physical training that pertains to any and every phase of combat. However, even newaza is not the final word in martial training.

For any aikidoka, his or her training is incomplete unless the true meaning of shugyo has been relentlessly pursued. Although shugyo is easily definable in words, its reality can elude us. Shugyo is the daily discipline of rigorous, passionate practice of aikido, in which what is learned on the mat influences our life outside the dojo. By challenging ourselves and questioning our ways of thinking, our spirits become refined. Passing beyond our fears, angers and need for acceptance, we reach toward enlightenment.

A shugyosha (practitioner of shugyo) follows the Way. Through dedication and perseverance in austere training, he or she improves cardio-pulmonary conditioning and optimizes brain function while elevating toward enlightenment. No special technique or manner of instruction by the sensei confers shugyo on the student. The sensei can lead and provide a climate in which shugyo can develop. Many of the hidden teachings in our aikido newaza are only secrets until they reveal themselves in practice. The techniques of both tachiwaza and newaza are different sides of the same coin. One emerges from the other. The truth is revealed only once the student is ready to see it. The shugyosha must discover the meanings of life's questions and answers for oneself. An aikidoka on the path of shugyo sets aside distractions such as partying and "seeking after shiny things" if they interfere with training.

O'Sensei considered shugyo to be an act of misogi, a way of cleansing the spirit. This esoteric practice has been considered to be an underlying theme in aikido and

Shinto. The aikidoka undergoes a purification of mind, body and spirit in order to harmonize with the order of the universe—it is a type of meditative practice. Misogi is first and foremost a quieting of the mind. In this state of receptivity, the shugyosha may be exposed to extreme temperatures. Possible examples could be standing under the cold water of a waterfall or sitting in a hot sauna. Less dramatic, cleaning the dojo is also misogi so long as a quiet mind is maintained. In fact, any repetitive practice performed in a state of mushin is misogi. Aikido is misogi.

Since we live very complicated lives in which work, family, and entertainment all vie for our time, some say that infrequent aikido training is better than none at all. Some students prefer to sleep and rest rather than train. Others make excuses and create illusionary diversions for why they cannot attend class. Some sensei can only teach once a week while others do not want the responsibility of running a dojo. So, there are probably few shugyosha among us. They are truly an endangered species in aikido. Maybe it is time to revive the spirit of shugyo, let go of self-imposed limits, set aside excuses and distractions, and aspire to be the best aikidoka within our reach.

Glossary

Ai-hanmi. – Triangular stance. Facing one another in identical stance

Aikido. – The Japanese martial art created by O'Sensei, Morihei Ueshiba. Aikido means "a way of life in harmony with ki, or the energy of the universe"

Aikido-ka. – A practitioner of aikido.

Aikido Kyogi. – Competitive aikido practice.

Aikidome. – A free flowing movement used in aikido during empty hand and weapons techniques to intercept, deflect and redirect the trajectory of an attack. An aikidome does not block or absorb the impact of a strike.

Aikijujutsu. – A Japanese martial art. Sokaku Takeda created Daito-Ryu aikijujutsu. It is the art with the most technical influence in the development of aikido.

Aiki ma-ai.– Immediate adjustment to time, space and conditions during any activity. Generally, it is thought as proper distance between nage and uke.

Aiki-newaza. – Ground grappling using aikido's harmonizing principles

Atemi. – Strikes.

Bajutsu. – The Japanese art of horsemanship.

Bojutsu. – The Japanese art of the staff.

Budo. – Martial arts and ways of Japanese life.

Budoka. – A practitioner of budo.

Bokken. – Wooden sword.

Bujutsu. – Combat techniques used by the warriors of ancient Japan.

Bukiwaza. – Weapons techniques.

Bushido. – The Samurai's code meaning "way of the warrior"

Chudan. – Middle level position.

Clinch. – The clinch is a transition that occurs from tachiwaza to newaza. A term often used in wrestling, boxing, muay thai, judo, jujutsu, MMA, etc., where one or both combatants grapple at close quarters in front or behind their opponent to prevent effective strikes, inhibit movement.

Daimyo. – Japanese feudal lord for the shogun.

Dan. – Instructor level rank.

Deai. – The moment of truth.

Deshi. – Student

Dojo. – Training hall

Domo arigato goziamasu. – A formal way to say "thank you very much"

Dozo. – "Please" or "please continue."

Ganseki-otoshi. – Rock drop throw.

Gedan. – Lower level position.

Gendai budo. – Modern martial ways.

Gi. – A martial arts uniform.

Gokyo. – Aikido's fifth classification or pinning technique.

Gyaku-hanmi. – Reverse half-body stance. Facing one another in opposite stance.

Hai. – Emphatic "yes."

Hajime. – The command to begin

Hakama. – A black skirt worn by black belt students as part of the formal uniform which adds an aesthetic beauty to aikido movements, used historically to protect a horseman's legs from brush while riding if not wearing armor.

Hanbo. – A three-foot stick.

Hanmi handachi. – Techniques where the attacker is standing and the defender is kneeling.

Hara. – The energetic and anatomical center of the body located a few inches below the navel

Helio Gracie. – The founder of Gracie Jiu-Jitsu

Henkawaza. – Variation techniques where one techniques flows into another.

Ikkyo. – Aikido's first principle technique.

Irimi. – An entering movement.

Iriminage. – Entering throw.

Jiyuwaza. – Freestyle technique.

Jo. – A four-foot wooden staff.

Jodan. – Upper level position.

Jo dori. – Techniques defending against the wooden staff.

Judo. – The Japanese martial art created by Dr. Jigoro Kano that evolved from jujutsu, later practiced as an Olympic sport.

Juji Gatame. – Cross pin.

Jujutsu. – The ancient Japanese martial art of throwing and grappling. Jujutsu means "gentle martial art"

Kaeshiwaza. – Countering techniques.

Kamae. – A posture or ready stance. In each kamae, there are different positions for the hand or weapon.

Kami shiho gatame. – Top four-corner hold.

Kansetsuwaza. – Joint-locking techniques.

Kaitennage. – Rotary throw.

Karate. – Or "empty hand," is a striking art that can also include various farm implement tools as weapons. There are many different systems that originate from Okinawa and Japan.

Kata. – A prearranged set of movements to simulate a combat situation.

Katana. – Japanese sword.

Katatedori. – One-handed wrist grab.

Katatedori ryote mochi. – Grabbing your partner's wrist with both hands.

Keiko. – Study or practice. The deeper meaning is "to return to the origin." Through the study and appreciation of the past, one can understand the present and therefore refine our spirit.

Kenjutsu. – The warrior art of the Japanese sword. These are the techniques utilized once the sword is deployed from the scabbard.

Keriwaza. – Kicking techniques.

Ki. – Internal energy.

Kiai. – Spirit yell.

Kodokan. – The martial arts headquarters for Dr. Jigoro Kano's judo. Kodokan translates to "practice way hall."

Kokyu. – The power of breath, renewal of life force.

Kokusai Budoin. – The International Martial Arts Federation.

Koryu. – Classical martial traditions.

Kosa dori. – Cross wrist grab (see also "ai hanmi katatedori.)

Koshi Nage. – Hip throw.

Kotegaeshi. – Wrist twist throw.

Kumi-Uchi. – An ancient Japanese grappling art.

Kuzushi. – To destroy one's balance.

Kumi Jo. – Paired jo practice.

Kumi tachi. – Paired sword practice.

Kyu. – Student level rank.

Kyudo/Kyujutsu. – The Japanese arts of archery.

Masakatsu agatsu. – True victory is self-victory.

Misogi. – Purification of mind, body, and spirit through ritualistic practices.

Modern Arnis – A progressive Philippine martial art created by Remy Amador Presas that included stick fighting and much more.

Mudansha. – Student (kyu) rank students

Mukei No Ryu. – The improvisational style of aikido developed by Jose Andrade-Shihan that translates to "system transcending form."

Munetsuki. – A straight punch to the abdomen or torso.

Mushin. – The philosophy of "no-mindedness."

Musubi. – This term means to tie. On a deeper meaning, opposites are different images of the same reality. Musubi is the process of their unification. It is the movement of the spiral.

Nage. – The person executing the technique.

Nagewaza. – Throwing techniques.

Newaza. – Ground techniques.

Nikyo. – Aikido's second principle technique.

Omote. – Life side angle.

Omoto-kyo. – The neo-shinto religion headed by Onisaburo Deguchi. This religion had a spiritual influence on Morihei Ueshiba's non-violent perspective of aikido.

Onisaburo Deguchi. – Spiritual leader of the Omoto-kyo religion that had the greatest spiritual influence on O'Sensei's aikido.

Osaewaza. – Pinning, holding and restraining techniques.

O'Sensei. - Great teacher. The title given to Morihei Ueshiba.

Randori. – Defense against multiple attackers.

Ronin. – A masterless warrior.

Ryu-Ha. – A martial arts style.

Samurai. – Japanese feudal warriors responsible for the advancement of many different martial arts. Samurai literally translates as "those who serve."

Sangen. - A multi-dimensional representation of the interactions of nature with humankind and, in like manner, interactions between two individuals during various phases of combat. The Sangen uses three fundamental geometric figures (triangle, circle, and square and their three-dimensional forms of pyramid, sphere, and prism) to represent the unity of mind, body and spirit, respectively.

Sankaku. – The triangular defensive position.

Sankyo. – Aikido's third principle technique.

Sato Shizuya. – One of Kokusai Budoin's founding members, chief director and grandmaster.

Sayuundo. – Sideways motion exercise.

Seiza. – Seated position.

Seppuku. – Ritual suicide by disembowelment.

Shihan. – Master level practitioner.

Shihonage. – Four winds throw.

Shikaku. – Blind side. It is a tactical position of being behind and very close to the attacker, also a position considered a prelude to the clinch.

Shikko. – Knee walking.

Shimewaza. – Choking techniques.

Shintoism. – A Japanese people's ethnic religion.

Shogun. – Japanese military commander.

Shomenuchi. – Strike to the top of the head.

Shoshin – Beginner's mind.

Shugyo. - The daily discipline of rigorous, passionate practice of aikido, where what is learned on the mat influences lives outside the dojo.

Shuhari. – Transcendence of tradition after long-term training.

Shurikenjutsu. – The Japanese art of throwing bladed objects.

Sogo Budo. – A composite martial art that expands the scope of one's training by integrating numerous martial ways within the framework of aikido. Morihei Ueshiba's aikido possesses the essential elements of each of the various other budo.

Sojutsu. – The Japanese art of the javelin or spear.

Suijutsu. – The Japanese art of swimming.

Suwariwaza. – Kneeling techniques.

Tachiwaza. – Standing techniques.

Taijutsu. – Empty hand techniques.

Takemusu aiki. – spontaneous movements drawing from the natural flow of energy in the universe.

Tanbo. – A two-foot wooden stick.

Tanden. – The hara, or center.

Tanren. – Techniques or exercises to develop proper movement of the hips.

Tanto. – Knife.

Tanto dori. – Techniques of knife defense (knife taking).

Tenchinage. – Heaven-and-earth throw.

Tenbinnage. – Elbow-lock throw.

Tenkan. – Calmed centered turning movements of the hips.

Tori. – See "nage"

Ude garami. – Arm entanglement.

Uke. – The one who receives. The person being thrown.

Ukemi. – Falling.

Ura. – Movement to the rear.

Ushiro kubi shime. – Rear choke used in aikido.

Ushirowaza. – Defenses where the attacks are from behind.

Wakizashi. – Japanese short sword.

Waza. – Technique.

Yame. – The command to stop.

Yokomenuchi. – Strike to the side of the body, most commonly to the temple, neck, and clavicle.

Yonkyo. – Aikido's fourth principle technique.

Yudansha. – Black belt (dan) rank holder.

Zanshin. – Continuity; remaining aware and prepared for the next action.

Zen. – The Japanese word for "meditation" as a way of existing without any goal or ulterior motive.

Blend with (ki-musubi) the

Universe of Heaven and Earth (tenchi)

Stand in the center of all

In your heart take up the stance

Of "The Way of the Mountain Echo"

Poetic Songs of the Way
Morihei Ueshiba (1883-1969)
Aiki News No. 46 March, 15, 1982

About The DVD:
Synopsis And Customer Reviews

Do you want to have the edge in your ground grappling skills? Would you like to add a new, effective and unique approach to your ground defense techniques that others are missing? Find out more about the power of the Mukei No Ryu aikido in this exciting, unprecedented, instructional DVD.

In this presentation, we cover a comprehensive abundant variety of classical aikido immobilizations such as ikkyo, nikkyo, sankyo, yonkyo, gokyo, and throws like shihonage, iriminage, kotegaeshi, koshinage, jujinage, kaitenage, sayuundo, tenbinage, tenchinage, kokyunage, and others. We also demonstrate a multitude of ground defenses designed for street survival. These include positions such as the guard, top mount, half mount, rear mount, cross mount, and scarf hold. Here we also show escapes, reversals, techniques against armed attacks, and submissions such as many different leg and arm chokes, arm and leg locks, sacrifice throws and much more. Please pay close attention and uncover the subtle hidden techniques that make Mukei No Ryu aikido a truly fascinating art.

HERE'S WHAT PEOPLE ARE SAYING ABOUT THE DVD:

"Aikido's Hidden Ground Techniques" is a must watch DVD not just once, but over and over again. It offers both a clinical and practical glimpse of the depth, power, and beauty of techniques rarely taught in aikido, the art of groundwork. Each time it's viewed, it will take you deeper and deeper into the art. For both the veteran aikido student and the beginning student alike, it's a must watch.

-David Blue has been studying the martial arts since 2009

My early exposure to Andrade Shihan's aikido was from his video, "Mastering your mind with aikido", released in 2000. Unlike the majority of modern aikidoka, who seem trapped in a maze of rigidly prescribed techniques, Andrade Shihan views aikido as an imaginative springboard that enables him to respond effectively to a diversity of self-defense scenarios in an aiki manner. His viewpoint is articulated well from this quote from the 2000 video: "Authentic aikido is not a collection of techniques. It is, rather, principles of nature, movement, and the power of the mind all put into action. Aikido is one spirit with infinite possibilities".

Andrade Shihan's latest DVD, "Aikido's Hidden Ground Techniques" produced in collaboration with David Nemeroff in 2017 is an eye-opening extension of that philosophy. Many martial artists would claim that "aikido ground-fighting" is an oxymoron. Yet, this DVD shows how the principles of effective ground fighting (newaza) have been present in historical aikido practice from O Sensei onwards (e.g., as seen in the cover photo). The fact that newaza has largely been ignored by modern aikidoka should not constrain our practice.

I view this DVD as showcasing several compelling and innovative responses to self defense ground-fighting scenarios. What makes it unique compared to other ground-fighting instructional videos is that Andrade Shihan's techniques are firmly grounded in aiki principles -- aikidoka will see familiar techniques applied in a newaza context as well as novel techniques that resonate with O Sensei's philosophy on aikido. I am reminded of two quotes in "The Art of Peace": "every encounter is unique, and the appropriate response should emerge naturally. Today's techniques will be different tomorrow. Do not get caught up in the form … The Art of Peace has no form" and "Absorb venerable traditions into this new Art … build on the classic styles to create better forms"

The reviewer, Dr. Rahul Sukthankar, has practiced Mukei No Ryu Aikido since 2007 and Shotokan Karate since 1991.

- Great Video! Demonstrates gentle adaptations to traditional aikido techniques when the attacks are not prearranged. Also, shows some options if your technique fails or if you lose balance during your execution, both of which often occur during a self-defense situation. For example, an attacker may grab you while you are executing an iriminage, which could bring you both to the ground. Or the attacker may spin out of a shihonage and tackle you to the ground. The video shows many examples like this and the instructors are able to improvise and maintain or regain control of the situation as it goes to the ground and beyond. Aikido principles of flow and using the attacker's energy against him occur throughout the video even when techniques have to be improvised beyond "traditional technique". The whole thing is Takemusu Aiki!

I still keep the Aikido Today Magazine article #51; Vol. 11, No. 1; April /May 1997 written by Andrade Shihan titled The Misinterpretation of Aikido's Essential Elements: A Personal View. Here are two essential quotes:

> *This is why Aikido is called "gentle." To many, gentleness suggest weakness. In fact, Aikido is so powerful that it has the potential for great harm which we must diligently strive to avoid on the mat. Off the mat, we sometimes have to choose whether to cause harm. We must remember that Aikido is an art of survival: when one is confronted with a life-or- death situation, one may have no choice but to use Aikido to survive. It is ignorance that leads some to deny that Aikido is a martial art that cannot inflict damage. (Of course, no martial art is 100% effective against all attacks).*

> *If Aikido is to survive, we must continue to preserve and pursue the teachings of O-Sensei. On the other hand, over the many years of my development in the martial arts, I have found it absolutely essential to change, adapt, and use modern methods and styles of instruction. In this way, I express the spirit of my teaching with vigorous and spontaneous creativity, unifying the traditional with the contemporary into one powerful art. In my dojo, I teach and practice with more emphasis on realistic attacks, focusing on practical self-defense – survival in "the concrete jungle." Some Aikido purists have said that what I teach is not Aikido. But, if is not Aikido, what is? Distancing ourselves from modern reality is not Aikido either. Aikido involves constant change – and this is one of its secrets.*

David Parker-Sensei

In my 50 years training in the martial arts years I have seen my share of books and video. Some good, some not so good and some outstanding. Shihans Andrade and Nemeroff's new DVD «Aikido's Hidden Ground Techniques» is an amazing depiction with application of how aikido principles can be applied to all areas of self-defense.

The focus of this video, aikido groundwork is like no other I have seen to this date. I really loved how the instructors give both cohesive instructional explanations of several techniques as well as a practical demonstration on how these techniques can be applied to real street combat.

I would recommend this dvd for anyone interested in seeing a unique and practical system of groundwork rarely taught in the aikido world. I give this video 5 stars and really think you should add this to your library when you have a chance. I highly recommend it.

Allie Alberigo-Shihan

About The Authors

Dr. Jose Andrade - Shihan

(aikitenshi@hotmail.com)

Dr. Jose Andrade - Shihan

Born February 3, 1953, Jose Andrade, MD, is a modern Zenman original. In 1966, he emigrated from Cuba with his parents and sister to the United States of America.

Dr. Andrade's interest in martial arts dates back to his childhood in Cuba. He began studying Nihon Goshin aikido in 1969 under Richard A. Bowe Shihan. He studied consistently in mainline aikido schools while cross-training in a diversity of other martial arts, such as wrestling, boxing, judo, jujitsu, kung fu, kobujutsu, karate, and filipino martial arts, from a variety of highly acclaimed teachers, including the late Grandmaster Remy A. Presas, founder of the International Modern Arnis Federation. In 1996, Andrade Shihan earned certification as instructor in advanced modern arnis under his tutelage.

Andrade Shihan founded Aikido Tenshinkai of Florida Inc. in 1995 in Orlando, Florida (www.aikitenshi.net). At this dojo he teaches aikido as a comprehensive martial art (sogo budo) to adults and children. His martial style is called Mukei No Ryu Aikido, or "style transcending form" aikido. This is a highly eclectic and improvisational type of aikido that encourages the participants to strive for Takemusu Aiki by directing the totality of their environmental exposures (exposome) towards survival, in harmony with aiki principles. The dojo also serves as a budokan -- home to many other martial arts -- beyond aikido, such as tai chi, judo, karate-do, kobudo and Nihon jujitsu.

In 2000, Andrade Shihan was inducted into the following three different martial arts halls of fame: the American Federation of Martial Arts Hall of Fame as National Instructor of the Year, the United International Kung Fu Federation as Sensei of the Year, and the World Head of Family Sokeship Council Martial Arts as Millennium Master Instructor.

In 2002, during the Kokusai Budoin/IMAF 50th Anniversary Commemorative Special Event, Andrade Shihan gave an aikido demonstration as part of the celebration of the 26th All Japan Budo Exhibition held at Hibiya Park in Tokyo, Japan. During this event the name Mukei No Ryu Aikido originated.

Andrade Shihan was among the thirty top martial arts instructors featured to perform a demonstration at the 8th Aiki Expo 2005 Friendship Demonstration at California State University, Dominguez Hills, Los Angeles, California. The event was hosted by the late Stanley A. Pranin, editor of Aikido Journal, respectfully known to Andrade Shihan as the Jose Marti of aikido, the national hero of Cuba. Andrade Shihan also taught aikido classes at the Aiki Expo 2005.

Andrade Shihan is Kyoshi, Shichidan (seventh dan) aikido. In 2010, his rank was granted directly from Kokusai Budoin Headquarters in Tokyo, Japan. He has studied and trained in Japan with Kokusai Budoin Masters of several different styles of aikido as well as in other budo. He views the healing arts, budo and aikido as immensely fulfilling and as a unified whole without conflict. As ambassador to Ueshiba's aikido, his budo emphasizes creativity, freedom and nonviolence. Inspired by O'Sensei's ideals, he is free from the patriarchal trappings of traditional Japanese Zen. He integrates his knowledge of the fundamental principles and values of budo and Zen applied to aikido into his adopted Western culture and his Cuban way of life.

He was presented a Community Service Award for his outstanding contributions and support to the Orlando, Florida, community by the Stop the Violence-Face the Music Society and No More Drugs Inc. He also participated in their "Street-Wise Drug Prevention" video presentation. Andrade Shihan wrote, produced and directed the videos, "Mastering Your Mind with Aikido" in 2000, "Aikido and Zen Secrets" in 2010, "Keriwaza and Newaza: Defense Applications" in 2012 and "Aikido's Hidden Ground Techniques" in 2017. In 2019, he authored the book Zen Steel, Aiki Heart/Aikido, Zen and the Quest for a Martial Way of Peace (Zen Steel Media).

In 2010, Gary S. Goltz, former president of the United States Judo Association (USJA), and the late Lowel F. Slaven, former USJA jujitsu chairman, appointed Andrade Shihan as chairman of the Aikido Division of this organization, where he served through 2016. He established the Aikido Committee/Promotion Board to preserve, teach and promote traditional aikido in the United States. Andrade Shihan is a member of the USJA Aikido and Jujitsu Committee Promotion Boards. He is also ranked Rokudan (sixth dan) in jujitsu from the USJA.

Dr. Jose Andrade graduated from the Universidad Central del Este Medical School in the Dominican Republic. Additionally, he has completed eight years of diverse university education in specialized and sub-specialized post-medical school training from the University of Medicine and Dentistry of New Jersey, Wayne State University, Emory University, and the University of South Florida.

Dr. Andrade has the rare distinction of being one of the few triple board recertified physicians in the United States, holding credentials granted by three different recognized and accrediting certifying boards of the American Board of Medical Specialties: the American Board of Pediatrics, Pediatric Rheumatology (sub-board of Pediatrics) and the American Board of Allergy and Immunology (a conjoint board of the American Board of Internal Medicine and the American Board of Pediatrics). Dr. Andrade is also a practitioner of acupuncture. He received this training from the University Miami School of Medicine, Miami, Florida. He is the clinical research principal Investigator for the Allergy Asthma and Arthritis Center of Central Florida. Dr. Andrade is a practicing physician with offices in Orlando and Kissimmee, Florida since 1987 (www.andrademd.com). In 2013, he made the top doctors list as compiled by the Washington, DC-based Consumers' Checkbook, a nonprofit organization. Dr. Andrade has contributed to the world of medical and martial arts literature with publications in journals and books. He is also a licensed real estate professional with interest in commercial real estate (andraderealestate@gmail.com). He enjoys the "delicate balance" between nature and foraging Florida's edible wild plants in his spare time.

David Nemeroff-Shihan

(www.aikido-dojo.com)

David Nemeroff originally hails from New York and currently resides in the Lehigh Valley near Allentown, PA. He began his martial arts journey at the age of seven years. However, he became more serious about his training at the age of twelve when he started practicing the art of Nihon Goshin Aikido. In order to complement his aikido regiment and become a more complete martial artist, Nemeroff added regular training in other martial arts such as jujutsu, kempo, iaijutsu and kenjutsu (samurai sword), kobudo (weapons), aikijutsu and others with Cary Nemeroff-Soke. To further expand his aikido education he was fortunate enough to also study various forms of aikido with different instructors from Kokusai Budoin, Tokyo, Japan, and find his current aikido instructor of over twenty-three years, Jose Andrade-Shihan.

David has a B.S. degree in fine arts with a graphic gesign specialization from Hofstra University. However, to better understand the human condition, he pursued the healing arts as well. In 2000, he became a licensed massage therapist, but he also focused on becoming trained in other modalities including craniosacral therapy (www.therapy4healing.com), foot reflexology, and essential oils, manual lymphatic drainage, Red Cross CPR, and first aid. He also has training in various qigong systems and is a professional member of the National Qigong Association.

Nemeroff-Shihan is now the director and chief instructor of Aikido Masters Self-Defense Academy in Whitehall, Pennsylvania. He has taught martial arts to people of all walks of life including law enforcement; military, corporations such as Air Products, St. Lukes Hospital, Penn State University and Mack Trucks; as well as children's organizations like the Boys and Girls Club of Allentown, Mosser Village Community Center, Camelot for Children, and Kid's Peace. He also teaches kempo to cancer survivors at the Cancer Support Community (a national non-profit organization). Currently, he has developed and implemented a martial arts program called the Kids Karate Project, which is specifically designed to help children afflicted with cancer and other special needs.

Nemeroff-Shihan's martial arts credentials include nineth dan – Fukasa-Ryu aikido, as well as dan ranks in Mukei No Ryu aikido, aiki-jo, and aiki-ken; aikido, Kokusai Budoin; Nihon Goshin aikido; Shihan in iaijutsu and kenjutsu (samurai sword); Shihan in kempojutsu; dan ranks in Hakatsuru kempo; jujutsu; aikijutsu, kobudo; one hundred hour certifications in jeet kune do, kali, and escrima; act 235 Lethal Weapons training instructor certification by the State of Pennsylvania, and certification as a defensive tactics instructor by United States specialized law enforcement training commission and the state of Pennsylvania.

Nemeroff has been featured on TV shows like the channel 69 news, TV-2 Sports Scene, Martial Arts TV online and various radio shows both nationally and internationally. He has also been in Aikido Today magazine as well as other publications. Nemeroff is also the author of three other books, Enter Into Aikido, I Can Learn Karate: Martial Arts First Steps for Kids and Modern Masters Of The Martial Arts: Actions and Insights Of The World's Classical Fighting Styles. He has also been in other books such as Mastering the Samurai Sword and Aiki-Jujutsu: Mixed Martial Art Of The Samurai.

His other accolades include being inducted and teaching aikido seminars at the Martial Arts Hall Of Honors in Atlantic City for several years in a row. However, the greatest reward to him is seeing how his students evolve and transform from his tutelage of the martial arts.

Though you may train

In this sword work or in that

What will it mean

Unless you do your utmost.

Poetic Songs of the Way
Morihei Ueshiba (1883-1969)
Aiki News No. 46 March, 15, 1982

Martial Arts Works by the Authors

Jose Andrade-Shihan

Mastering Your Mind With Aikido (DVD)

Aikido and Zen Secrets (DVD)

Keriwaza and Newaza: Defense Applications (DVD)

Zen Steel, Aiki Heart. Aikido, Zen and the Quest for a Martial Way of Peace – To be published

David Nemeroff-Shihan

Enter Into Aikido

I Can Learn Karate: Martial Arts First Steps For Kids

Modern Masters of the Martial Arts: Actions and Insights of the World's Classical Fighting Systems

www.ingramcontent.com/pod-product-compliance
Lightning Source LLC
Chambersburg PA
CBHW081328090426
42737CB00017B/3055